ABOUT THE AUTHOR

Poppy Delbridge is a mind coach, speaker and tapping expert. She has worked with major networks, including the BBC, ITV, Channel 4 and Netflix, and was named 'one of the most powerful women in TV' by *Glamour*. Poppy has since founded the personal development community, House of Possibility, which encourages people to realise their own power and potential. By sharing her unique Rapid Tapping® methodology, Poppy has helped chief executives of Fortune 100 companies, CBEs and CEOs upgrade their ordinary to move effortlessly into extraordinary success. *Tapping In* is Poppy's first book. She splits her time between London and the Cotswolds.

Dear Marie,

"It is done that my money project got completed quickly, effortlessly + joyfully"

Poppy xx.

POPPY DELBRIDGE

Tapping in

**MANIFEST THE LIFE
YOU WANT WITH
THE TRANSFORMATIVE
POWER OF TAPPING**

PIATKUS

PIATKUS

First published in Great Britain in 2022 by Piatkus

3 5 7 9 10 8 6 4 2

A CIP catalogue record for this book is available from the British Library.

ISBN 978-0-3494-3176-5

Typeset in Garamond by M Rules
Printed and bound in Great Britain by Clays Ltd, Elcograf S.p.A.

Papers used by Piatkus are from well-managed forests and other responsible sources.

Piatkus
An imprint of
Little, Brown Book Group
Carmelite House
50 Victoria Embankment
London EC4Y 0DZ

An Hachette UK Company
www.hachette.co.uk

www.littlebrown.co.uk

To the man who made me believe, and
his grandson who made me a mother.

TABLE OF CONTENTS

INTRODUCTION

Let's begin our tapping transformation ...

You're not really here to learn about tapping, are you? You're actually here to discover how you can manifest your wildest possibilities. So what is it that you want to achieve? Fortunately, it just so happens that tapping is an unexpectedly simple gateway to accomplishing the life you have always wanted – to making your ultimate life a reality.

What many of us don't realise is that we are already working towards this, 24/7 – and also that we can guide energy negatively, as well as positively. We create opportunities based on our emotions – and if those are primarily feelings of tension, stress and pain, directing energy towards them will simply amplify our distress. So if you don't absolutely love your current reality, you've got to change the way you show up; you've got to change what you believe about yourself and your potential. But I'm not here to tell you we can simply *think* things into being – if we could, we'd all be in Bali sipping cocktails, yet doing nothing to make that happen. Instead, what I give my clients – and now you – is a tangible, make-it-happen creative process that delivers evidence-backed results to allow you to receive what's always been there, just waiting for you. I know you're ready for the next level.

Anything is possible with tapping – I've seen it with my own eyes. I've read the research papers, witnessed the transformations in my clients – and allowed the practice to change my own life quite dramatically, year on year. It never gets boring and it never lets me down. The only drawback I've come across is that we can under-estimate the benefits of tapping because it's so unnervingly simple.

Notice I said simple – not easy. Even though I'll share straight-forward and step-by-step methods to manifest your goals in this book, it's hard to stick to the practice unless you understand the science behind it, the magic of it, how it affects our cognition, when to apply it and what it will bring to you.

It's all too easy to want to change your life isn't it? – but next-level change involves working on yourself, which can sometimes be scary, or feel like a drag. But you've picked up this book and I honour you for that: I'm on a mission to make your transform-ation as fun and wide-reaching as I can. Doing the inner work but remaining playful and curious about your future possibilities is what tapping is all about. You're going to start playing with energy, and I'll guide you on your journey to creating a life that you down-right love. Every aspect – your career, your relationships, your sex life, your financial well-being, your home environment, your physical and emotional health – deserves to be the best it can be.

And the cool part? The particular methodology I will share with you is rapid, long-lasting and relies on a clinically proven set of techniques.

My heartfelt intention (I'm big on these, as you'll discover) is that you will begin to flirt with all the possibilities that exist for you *right now*. The more you believe in possibility, the more your negative thought-loops, objections and limiting beliefs about both yourself and the wider world will lose power. Do the beliefs hold-ing you back even belong to you? Or are they someone else's? Once you've broken free from what's holding you back, we will take it further. This is about actively stepping into your most powerful self to create a wild future that you can't wait to meet.

Curious? I certainly hope so. Embrace this positivity.

We're all prone to letting the negatives drown out the positives – we're often so used to our perceived limitations that we become blind to possibility. But it's out there and you can have more than a 'meh' kind of life. Coping, settling, waiting, procrastinating or second-guessing yourself doesn't offer you inner peace and it isn't empowering. And even if your life is fabulous right now, and you love yourself to bits, it can always be upgraded. To supercharge yourself and step into what I like to call a 'hi-life', I will help you tap into a new life-navigation system: the way of creative man-ifestation. In this state of flow you will finally feel aligned, free and powerful.

Still sceptical? Well, I'm going to be vulnerable now, so you can understand why I'm so passionate about tapping – and why I *know* you can transform your own life no matter where you are now.

This next part that you're about to read – my personal story – I rewrote at the eleventh hour. I had originally included a pared-back version that I'd hesitantly shared with my partner. His response to it surprised me: 'Is that it? It's not emotional at all.'

Reading my words back, he was right. I'd written down my own experience in a mechanical, apologetic way – a sign that I had been avoiding a chance to heal an emotional block of my own. So the day my editor needed the final manuscript back, I cried. I sat and tapped on my own shame. I had avoided expressing what had happened to me for so many years that sitting and writing it all down overwhelmed me with a strong sense of both relief and sadness. I'm about to tell you the truth of why I started tapping.

It's February 2010. 'Surprise!' Everyone is gathered in the pub, when me, my son and my husband walk in. A shout of 'Happy Birthday!' rings out. It's my husband's birthday and I've arranged this whole thing. I haven't slept but nobody knows I'm exhausted. Everyone thinks I'm the same old, fun, happy Poppy, and that we're the perfect couple with the sweet son, nice home and cool jobs. I haven't slept because adrenalin has kept me awake. My husband slept-talked in the night and it made me sick.

Intuitively, I'd already known what had been going on, but I went ahead with the party anyway. Nobody suspected our ten-year marriage was about to fall apart. Nobody knew that my entire identity was being stripped away from me – and how completely alone I felt. I was stuck in my own 'success'. I went to sleep that night knowing that everything was about to change.

A few days later I woke up in agony, although this time it was physical. I went to the bathroom and noticed that one of my eyes was bloodshot. Then the other one was too. By the evening my entire face was burning and blotchy. Soon I couldn't see. In the eye hospital, I went through the MRI scans with doctors, desperate to find out what was causing the pain. I was told that I was going blind. But still he went to band practice instead of staying at home to take care of me. So, I sat alone and listened to audiobooks while my heart shattered into tiny pieces – but now I know that this was my turning point.

I've always been interested in spirituality, but it was while I was in physical and emotional agony that I finally listened to Rhonda Byrne's *The Secret* for the first time. I fell down a rabbit hole and soon enough, I'd listened to several other books on metaphysics. I was being invited to transform and I had no physical option other than to surrender. Disgusted and paralysed by fear I soon uncovered the truth of what had happened right in front of my eyes: he was having affairs. He was not the man I'd married. I was betrayed, I felt stupid and I blamed myself immediately. This was my fault. I wasn't good enough. I must have spent too much time on my career, or with my son. I was a bitch – a terrible wife.

Suddenly, I was no longer the playful go-getter that everyone thought I was. Who was I then? I realised that I had been pretending to be happy and positive for a very long time, when really I'd been desperately lonely in my relationship. I began this cycle of 'negative selfing' – self-blame, self-loathing, anything that meant it was my fault, my fuck-up. In the space of a few weeks, the life that I knew had mutated into something unrecognisable. I felt like a failure and a fraud; and the shame (and the stress) was so shocking, so all-encompassing, so traumatic that I believe it physically blinded me. I decided that I needed to change my life. My eyes healed – quite miraculously actually – a physical sign of my transformation? I had no idea at the time that I was being divinely guided towards a set of tools that would transform my life beyond my wildest dreams.

I can still remember the night he finally admitted everything and told me he didn't love me any more. I was wearing a vest top, but still I cried in the street for hours while it rained. The next day I went into work on autopilot. My boss was understanding, and I took a sabbatical to Cornwall to see my mum. I didn't eat for a week. I was in a state of severe shock. On the train to my mum's, I started journalling my thoughts and tried to use manifestation to lift my mood, but nothing was helping me emotionally.

'Tap with me, Poppy,' my mum said.

Mechanically, I started tapping with and repeating after her – unsure if it would have any effect on me. Within minutes, I felt noticeably calmer. The raging ball of anger, pain and sadness inside me began to dissipate and I felt lighter, soothed – through tapping I became a version of myself that I hadn't met for years. I felt like *me* again. I want to show you that no matter what has happened or how you feel – it's possible to transform your life. And it won't take as long as you think when you use tapping.

Whenever I reflect on my journey back to my truest self, this quote by Brené Brown always feels so apt:

'We don't want our sadness overlooked or diminished by someone who can't tolerate what we're feeling because they're unwilling or unable to own their sadness.'

If you've come to terms with owning your own emotions, or you're intending to by the end of this book, then you might feel ready to ask yourself these audacious questions:

- What if I can own my sadness but I want to access a higher vibration of joy?
- In a world of suffering, can I live a happy life?
- Is envisioning more for my life being ungrateful for what I currently have?
- Am I even allowed to radiate joy and manifest what I want?

I don't have all the answers – and if you are avoiding your own sadness, pain and demons this book may not be for you. But if you're ready to move towards all the joy, pleasure, bliss and ecstasy that is awaiting you in an infinite, abundant universe ... then you're in the right place. I've got you. I have devoted my life to asking bold questions about living life in the energy of pure possibility – and here and now I would like to confirm that living joyfully is possible. In ALL areas of your life.

Through experiencing the deepest depths of my own pain, I have learned that the quality of my life does not depend on external factors. I've also learned that our capacity for receiving and attracting more of what we want can be raised with certain energy-based techniques and practical exercises. Tapping is my number one way to shortcut your journey to joy.

When I realised my high-flying media job wasn't ultimately bringing me joy, I chose to leave it. I was good at it, but it wasn't making my heart sing so I listened to my intuition and took a leap into the unknown. I now enjoy multiple creative pursuits: developing ideas, nurturing talented leaders and speaking on international stages about tapping, manifesting and creativity. I love delivering courses and workshops, and my mission is to liberate people from the things that are holding them back from their brightest possibilities. I have my own podcast, *Rapid Tapping*, an app that I self-funded and the chance to write this book. I also run a private members' club for manifestors, House of Possibility, where hi-life seekers all over the world can come home to themselves and their fullest potential. I have my wonderful son, and I'm in an incredible relationship with a man I love.

For years I questioned whether I was even allowed to live a life in this kind of joy, but my soul kept coming back at me: how dare you *not* live a life of joy! So every day I give myself permission to choose joy again, no matter what. And you must do the same. Because when you make that decision, you empower not just yourself but your family, your friends, your communities. You create a ripple effect for radiating joy.

This is not just a book about how to live your life joyfully, confidently and successfully. This is a book that can change the world – if you decide to change yours.

Let's begin tapping in.

PART ONE

Clear

Imagine that you're standing on the edge of a cliff. Ahead of you is a bridge and on the other side of that bridge is a place of abundance and joy. As you take your first steps forward, you're full of beans. In the vague distance you can see land, but as you continue along the bridge a fog descends, shrouding everything with mist. Your initial enthusiasm wanes and your doubt takes over. It's getting dark too. You begin to ask yourself, 'Why am I even on this bridge?'

'You wanted to cross the bridge, didn't you?'

'I think so, but it's harder than I thought it would be. I don't know any more.'

'Keep going . . .'

'Or maybe I should just wait it out for a bit? The fog might clear.'

'Walk on – it'll be worth it.'

'It's taking too long, I'm scared. I'll just head back – at least it's familiar.'

But by turning back you never get to see what happens. This kind of inner dialogue is exactly what stops you from getting to where you want to be. You might try to cross this bridge – or other metaphorical bridges – again, and again, and again.

When moving into positive experiences in our relationships, career, well-being and finances, we often find that there's a bridge involved that separates us from reaching our destination. If you want to manifest a specific, positive outcome, you might find that the bridge can play out in two ways: either you stay on it freaking out and unable to move forward, or you retreat back to what you're used to. Even though you know a life of abundance is waiting for you on the other side. But there's a third option too: tapping can help to remove the bridge altogether.

In Part One of this book, I'm going to help you pave a safe, clear and rapid pathway to successful manifestation by mastering tapping – and more specifically how to use it to 'clear'. Picture yourself on the bridge again, but this time you're able to see through the mist, to calm your mind and ease your fear. Instead, imagine if you could redirect all the wasted energy you used up by fretting on the bridge? Imagine if you could be done with living in limbo. Now you can. In the next few chapters, I'm going to share with you how tapping works, why I use it to manifest and how to master the basics to set you on a new journey of self-discovery and next-level living. I'll introduce you to the different states of consciousness we can hack into, how to reduce overwhelm with a life-zoning system called the 'Wheel of Possibility', and we'll even create an overarching vision for your future.

Often, you might catch yourself reflexively thinking 'that's just the way things are' or 'that's how we're programmed', when it's not actually true. Ask yourself: what would be possible if I tweak my mindset and my energy? More. Part One of this book will come alive for you if you can stay alert and gently question the things you've always believed to be true.

1 TAPPING INTO MORE

'If your mind is empty, it is always ready for anything; it is open to everything. In the beginner's mind there are many possibilities, in the expert's mind there are few.'

SHUNRYU SUZUKI, ZEN BUDDHIST

Having found your way to this book, we are now on the path to accessing infinite and unthinkable possibilities *together*. Welcome aboard. Things are going to get vibey. Weird, even. You're going to be challenged and confronted; excited and euphoric. I certainly felt all of those emotions while writing this.

As a coach and strategist I've worked with thousands of clients, from A-list celebrities to Fortune 100 chief execs, from CBEs to CEOs, from psychologists to neuroscientists. I've advised emerging UK start-ups and the biggest creative companies in the world about manifestation and mindset. When it comes to success, I advocate a more holistic, multi-passionate view of what that means for each person. As well as being a BAFTA judge and chair with a long career in television media, specialising in creative development, I'm also a certified practitioner in Neuro Linguistic Programming (NLP), reiki, Ericksonian hypnosis and energy psychology. But rather than being the expert, I'm coming to you as a friend and beginner because we all fuck up sometimes. But as Norman Vincent Peale, the godfather of positive vibration said, 'Become a possibilitarian. No matter how dark things seem to be or actually are, raise your sights and see the possibilities – always see them, for they're always there.'

Living the life of a joyful possibilitarian requires us to continually go beyond the surface and dig deeper. Psychologists now believe that we have around six thousand thoughts a day, but only a small percentage of these are conscious. When it comes to what we *think* we know about our potential, we really operate on the tip of a whopping big iceberg. Most of what we experience (and expect) in life is coloured by how our minds have been programmed – all those conscious and subconscious cues absorbed from family, friends and society since birth, then cemented by media stereotypes, the people we spend time with or where we live. My job is to empower you to question your limits because, well, are they limits? Or do you just think they are? When it comes to the whole gamut of transformational energetic work, like tapping, you're probably in the dark. This is not stuff they teach you at school.

I want you to ask yourself: what do you *truly* want? You may not know yet and that's OK because we will get into this later. But no matter what it is, the next step to achieving it is to understand your unique 'coding'. We all have an energetic imprint and this 'coding' keeps running behind the scenes, rather like code on your laptop, doing its job on repeat until it's time for an upgrade. Your old piece of code hasn't received that memo from you yet, has it? The one that says: *Hell yes – I am able to go further, bigger, deeper than ever before, no matter what.*

To do that, you and I will uncover your positive desires and confront what I refer to as 'the gremlins', the nasties hidden inside your energetic wiring that keep you from having the life you want. Your coding is a blueprint of judgements, emotional attachments and past evidence that bruises your ability to manifest joyfully and effectively. It becomes the reason you feel like something probably won't happen for you. It makes you feel insecure, stuck, unworthy and incapable. And, spoiler alert, I'm afraid we are all human so we can't eliminate fear completely, ever. But as you'll find out, inside every gremlin is the beautiful whisper of a hopeful, healed existence, of the ability to finally be who you want to be and to unlock a next level. Even if you are already incredibly happy or successful and you're reading this book to improve your professional or personal landscape, you may not realise quite how wild and big things could be for you . . . yet.

WHAT IS TAPPING?

First off, it seems silly. Tapping on specific, invisible 'points' on your body to truly connect to your emotions – *really*? Yes. It works. I won't pretend I wasn't slightly sceptical at first, but however strange it might seem it works *so* well and *so* rapidly that I'm a complete convert. I really don't care if someone sees me tapping in public: I've done it in fancy restaurants, in busy supermarkets, in taxis. I've had clients tapping on trains to help them concentrate while writing reports, at the school gates to remain calm as their kid screams, and in the toilets at work to boost confidence before meetings. I've used tapping to heal my emotional and even physical pain and to strategically manifest what I want for myself: like unshakeable confidence, grounding self-belief and even a brilliant sex life.

'Tapping' is a blend of traditional energy medicine and modern clinical cognitive methods. There are many different approaches to the practice, with evidence of humans first tapping on their bodies as a form of self-soothing as far back as five thousand years ago. You may be familiar with the Eastern practice of acupuncture, where practitioners place needles strategically on the body to help ease recurring pain and tension. When used in the right way, acupuncture can help to promote peak health and allow vital *c'hi* (*qi*) energy to flow in perfect balance. A no-needle version of the practice, acupressure, developed all the way back in 6000 BC and involved locating bodily acupoints with sharpened stones. In the last few decades, this method has helped alleviate issues like motion sickness and headaches, and to promote overall wellbeing – but it wasn't until the introduction of psychology that what we've come to understand as tapping was born.

It was American psychologist, Dr Roger Callahan, who first thought to combine the two fields in 1980. With a keen interest in Eastern energy techniques, Dr Callahan decided to try using tapping as a form of therapy for his clients to balance out their emotional disturbances. Encouraged by a number of successes – including his ability to cure a water-phobic patient – Dr Callahan applied his techniques to a range of traumas and found that tapping could help dislodge negative thoughts and behaviours. This radical new approach to healing was initially referred to as Thought Field Therapy (TFT).

Advancements in TFT allowed the practice to develop into something even simpler, yet no less effective, with a student of Dr Callahan's, Gary Craig, pioneering a new form of therapy known as Emotional Freedom Techniques (EFT) in the 1990s, which you may have heard of, or used. Over the years several different approaches to tapping have evolved, including Karl Dawson's matrix reimprinting, which centres on our inner child and how we can heal childhood trauma, and Steve Wells's Simple Energy Techniques (SET).

I am a certified practitioner of the EFT method so everything I advise in this book will relate to my understanding of tapping from years of advanced-level training and practice with clients in EFT. As a former Warner Bros Executive, with a career in creative leadership, development and strategy within global television companies and broadcasters, I have a wealth of experience working with data, people and new ideas, and I'm naturally interested in pushing the boundaries of what is possible. My own curiosity was piqued as soon as I saw how tapping could be developed further to help us manifest the lives we want. I see tapping as a limitless practice that has so much more to offer.

It's backed by science but founded by the Universe. It's proven that tapping can swiftly reset, neutralise and de-stress, but as a manifest-ation coach, I wanted to see what other benefits it could provide. This led to me developing my own technique that's perhaps the first to take a dual manifesting–tapping approach: 'Rapid Tapping'. I've had my particular methodology kindly referred to by the press as 'positive tapping', or 'manifestation tapping', because it helps you feel and achieve more of what I call the 'good stuff'. But make no mistake, if you want to create more you'll need to clear out blocks – and we all have those. If even showing up each day can feel like a challenge, (and I've been there, I feel you) I want to invite you to join me in a vibration of hope. My Rapid Tapping protocols are a set of easy-to-use and surprisingly short routines based on the law of attraction and a blend of neuroscience and 'new science', which we'll explore later.

'Rapid' in this context refers to the speed of transformation you can achieve, rather than the pace at which you tap your fin-gers (note that I'm not encouraging you to be Speedy Gonzales). It's also about how quick in duration the tapping routines are.

Traditionally, tapping has been carried out in one-to-one sessions with clients over sixty- to ninety-minute sessions, but I also advocate a daily, shortened self-led practice that will help to elevate your well-being in anything from thirty seconds to fifteen minutes.

We live in a busy world where it's not always an option to visit a practitioner, so part of my mission is to offer accessible energy techniques that can be incorporated seamlessly into your life and carried out at home or on the go. I'll offer up the exact routines I designed for modern, curious and forward thinkers like you to help manifest everything from promotions to establishing a successful business, from finding a soulmate to mending broken relationships, and everything in between.

Big talk there, huh? You may have tried goal-setting before, but to do so without tapping is leaving a whole lot of potential on your table. Achieving goals is part psychological and part embodiment. Once you combine the two, you'll be able to access new pools of untapped energy, and you'll stop wasting energy on unseen emotional blocks that keep you from having what you want and feeling the way you want to.

WHAT IS ENERGY PSYCHOLOGY?

I'm completely fascinated by the whole spectrum of energy psychology – of which tapping is a major part – because of the seemingly miraculous effect it has on my clients (and, of course, on me). So although tapping plays a major role, this book teaches you how to use energetic manifestation first and foremost.

Dr David Feinstein, a clinical psychologist and respected researcher within the energy psychology field, explains it well:

*'Energy psychology is an umbrella term for treatment
approaches that incorporate an energetic component into the
psychotherapeutic process. The stimulation of acupuncture
points (acupoints) by tapping on them is the most widely
used and well-investigated intervention distinguishing
the approach.*

You don't need to know huge amounts about points or the
meridian lines to use tapping; the real trick to tapping is to accept
that energy is at the heart of everything. When I discovered how
deep this goes, crossing over with the mystical, metaphysics, quantum mechanics and psychology, I started seeing life in a whole new
light. Dr Feinstein is also the husband of the formidable Donna
Eden, a spokesperson and pioneer of energy medicine, whose
energy techniques have been healing people all over the world for
four decades. Together, I have a little crush on them.

WHAT EXACTLY IS ENERGY?

From *prana* in India and *ch'i* (*qi*) in China, to *holy spirit* in
Christianity and *mana* in Polynesian culture, the idea of energy
exists in cultures, religions and movements the world over. I believe
that there is, at the very heart of all, a Truth: an existence of infinite
and incredible Universal Energy. This is so grand and great that
we cannot really begin to understand it, so we label it to get our
heads around it. Tapping is a way to work with this energy, rather
than against it. It's really on our side, but we haven't been taught
how to tap into it yet – or worse, it's been dismissed as a woo-woo
mystical practice. But this presupposes that energy is the antithesis

of rational thinking, which is manifestly untrue. Just have coffee with a quantum physicist and get back to me on that.

It's wise to remember that although as a society we're constantly making scientific and technological advances, we don't always have the tools at our disposal to prove *why* something works. Often, we find phenomena in the universe that we cannot yet explain, and we are quick to criticise when we don't understand *how* something works. An example we can point to is aspirin, which can be traced back to the anti-inflammatory willow leaf as early as 3000 BC, yet it only became one of the world's most researched drugs many civilisations later. We tappers know that tapping is only just getting started.

Tapping allows us to safely and quickly shift trapped energy in our bodies, stored over many years of memories – and it's natural. It's *energy*. Energy needs to flow, move, shift and release, all day long.

HACK: Think about your own ugly memories. It is impossible to think about a memory without some kind of emotional response. That's an energy that you're holding.

We're not taught that it's perfectly OK and even *necessary* to release the energy of an emotion in the moment (big girls don't cry and all that rubbish), let alone tap when it happens so the emotional charge doesn't affect our overall frequency. Emotions are energy in motion but we leave them in our personal long-stay car park, year after year, and compound a sense of ingrained anger, frustration or sadness. Trapped energy will stay in place for years, festering away – and it will negatively impact your actions, behaviour and personality. Not to mention your health. But this book is going to change all that.

THAT THING I DO CALLED TAPPING

I'm allergic to self-care 'fluff': advice that tells you how easy it is to change overnight just by taking an aromatherapy bath, or that by thinking nice 'manifesting' thoughts, you will receive nice things in return. At best this sort of advice will buy you some time; at worst it's toxic. Nobody needs more 'have a bubble bath, take a break, buy another candle' nonsense without actual, practical root change. Those things *are* nice, but they won't deliver you the kind of stable, inner peace that we're all after. Neither will they bring you the unshakeable self-belief and self-worth needed to live the lifestyle you want. Enjoying a lovely day at the spa, but still dwelling in the impossibility of your future dreams while you're there is placing attention on the wrong thing. It's empty self-care.

If you're anything like me, you have shit to do – and you want results. And you want them fast. I'm going to teach you about the power of focus, how to get into total flow state, and how to feel better fast. In my career I have been responsible for multi-million-pound budgets and managed teams of men twice my age, all the while trying to navigate life as a single mother to my son; I know what it is to juggle, to be overwhelmed, to be swamped by stress. Tapping was my lifeline when I didn't believe I was *enough* on a daily basis. I know what it's like to feel that you're failing in life, even when you're doing everything in your power to be a success. I know that gnawing sense of shame when people assume you have it all, but all you want to do is hide under the duvet and make the world stop.

More than that, though, tapping is now your 'supercharger' tool to become more productive, more fulfilled and more *you*.

> **HACK:** happiness is not something that's static; neither should you expect it to be. But humans are not designed to live in a state of constant anxiety either.

A life of contentment is possible if we apply the right techniques and tap into a new paradigm. Sure, we'll all have our emotional ups and downs, experience crap days and occasionally want to stab a colleague with a pen, but I am not in the business of just helping you cope. I'm here to shift you into a state of true, infinite and exciting abundance – and I'm loud and proud about that.

WHAT CAN YOU USE TAPPING FOR?

Absolutely everything, actually. Tapping is used all over the world by clinical practitioners to treat a whole range of concerns: stress, insomnia, headaches, pain relief, weight loss, depression, PTSD, phobias, anxiety, anger issues, addiction, chronic fatigue, relationships, financial abundance, peak performance and more.

I focus mainly on the fairly new realm of 'creating', aka manifesting with tapping. This is not to be confused with tapping your body while saying random positive affirmations, which I don't think is going to get you anywhere fast (I'll explain why later). What I want to outline is a simple 'clear to create' method: if we want to create something in our lives, we need to first clear some stuff out. Logic tells us this, but it also applies to our energy system and the emotions we carry. Pivoting your mindset into one of power and proactivity is my thing, and there seems to be no limit to what tapping can do when applied to manifestation principles.

In the courses I teach and the memberships I run, I've seen the tangible manifestations of money; miracle babies; jobs and joy; physical healings and phobic recoveries.

PUTTING TAPPING INTO PRACTICE

I get passionate throughout this book. I might even swear. Shit, I already have, haven't I? I know my passion may polarise people, but, look, we are all humans here, trying our best to break free from our own limitations, so when I see someone being held back from their right life, it gets me worked up. Because I *know* you can make the impossible possible if you have the right process; the right alchemy. I *know* you can feel better and dream bigger by tapping in with me. But . . . you have to show up for me too!

Psychoanalyst Carl Jung said, 'You are what you do, not what you say you'll do.' This is true, isn't it? How often do we confuse buying a book about self-development with actually doing the exercises it suggests? I've had swanky cookbooks on my shelves for years, and it gives me a false sense of being a master chef! I'm not. But if I put some effort into actually trying out the recipes, I would have the capacity to become a master chef. Or if I wanted to become a pilot, I could become one with enough practice and direction.

HACK: Please remove the word 'try' from your vocabulary. Trying suggests that it's not actually happening. It's as flimsy as a summer smock. If my son is going to miss his school bus, I don't try to get in my car. I take the necessary steps to make sure he gets to school on time. I get in the car, start the engine, indicate. Shit gets done when you get determined.

Part of my role here is to stress how important it is to actually *implement* these tapping techniques regularly. If you aren't committed to your practice, you won't experience the change or result you're after.

If it's not impossible, it's possible

Tapping enabled me to reinvigorate my life; to accept and acknowledge my emotions. I felt an abrupt shift from negative to positive on the contentment scale – and I've never looked back. When you stop thinking with just your head and become attuned to your energetics, something cool happens – you shift. By introducing short and punchy Rapid Tapping routines and exercises into your life, bit by bit, tap by tap, you will feel the energetic and emotional attachments unhooking from you one by one, until you heal and can really begin creating magic.

There's a ton of mysterious jazz going on that our human brains can't begin to fathom. Our intentions, affirmations and energetic coding are nothing short of miraculous. Miracles are happening all the time, yet we are taught to focus on the impossibility rather than the possibility of them. Even if you believe it's impossible to shift your life up a gear right now I have to tell you that you've been lied to. You can learn to regulate your emotions, set yourself free from many of them, understand how to play with energy and take back control.

And when you do that:

- You can stop being so hard on yourself.
- You can stop reacting when colleagues trigger you.
- You can remain cool when your partner annoys you.
- You can say no to people who pull you down.
- You can glide over your parents' cutting remarks.
- You can feel good about your body.
- You can lose and fail and stay positive.
- You can let your children make their own mistakes.
- You can stay calm when all around you lose their heads.
- You can stop self-sabotaging.
- You can master yourself.
- You can do whatever you want to do and be whoever you want to be.

WE NEED A 'HIGHER' GAME PLAN

You have a part to play as the executive producer of your own life; if you're acting as a bystander rather than a main player you need to take full responsibility and reclaim your power! You can't control other people, because that's exhausting and too many of them are a pain in the ass – you can, though, control *you*. Will you choose to be the master of your reactions, responses, emotional state and behaviours?

> **HACK:** If you've ever found meditation difficult – because clearing your mind isn't your forte – you can use tapping to relax into meditation, or help remain focused by actively tapping on any drifting thoughts as they show up during your practice.

In order to create our ultimate life, I believe that we need a higher understanding. I want you to know the basics of how science and spirituality cross over to deliver exponential results. We'll start by understanding the principles of quantum physics, the workings of the brain and some spiritual strategies in relation to tapping. You want to manifest your wildest vision, right? The one you haven't yet dared to dream up? OK – then we lean into 'out of the box' ways of thinking, and get creative. Your lowest self cannot produce your highest results and being willing to choose a different way of navigating life is crucial. But even though I can be almost evangelical about this 'higher power' or 'higher self', this is a guide to developing your own understanding of the universe, not mine. I couldn't care less if you call your higher power the Universe, God, Source or Sarah – all I ask is that you come to this book with an open mind and a whole heart. It goes much further than a technique to keep you calm. When you want to manifest, you're dealing with the divine.

Imagine for a minute ...

Go on – just imagine and daydream what might be possible for you for one minute. You see, imagination is necessary if you want to pioneer change in your life.

We wouldn't have anything without imagination. The scientists of past times just kept on being curious, kept learning, kept persisting, kept imagining. They didn't give up and say, 'Right, that'll do. This is it.' They didn't ever say, 'This theory is too good to be true, let's forget about it.' And just imagine if they had! We'd have no microwaves for a start – and my uncle literally wouldn't be able to eat.

Take a moment and think about how you are only in the

preview of your life, not the ending. What does the next chapter look like? The story you see as your 'life' hasn't entirely played out yet. The story that you tell yourself, that seems so real, has been constructed from the way you've been brought up. You see, things you've been conditioned to believe can stunt your imagination and affect the way you approach the future. Everything you've seen at the cinema, all those things your parents said about you, the education you received, the heartbreak you experienced, the limits you unconsciously applied to your potential, all colour your unique perception of what is currently possible. But the beginning of a story is not the same as the end, and you have the ability to edit the ending as you like – and to keep creating new beginnings.

We are hardwired as humans to accept what we think, feel and see to be the cold hard truth, but I'll lay foundations with you to unpick the false truths that are keeping your potential rigidly stuck under a glass ceiling, withholding the open sky above.

'What is now proved was once only imagined.'

WILLIAM BLAKE, poet

A massive part of this book is about imagining what *could* be as well as tackling what *is*. And if your imagination is limited right now, that's OK – just remember to be open to possibility. If we tap into the resonance of possibility, we access potential proven versions of ourselves, latent and ready to burst forth.

HACK: Your life will change if you focus on accepting that we don't need to be 'perfect' or 'the finished article'. Nothing is impossible: we are just living to impossible standards. There will always be things we can't prove, feelings we don't understand and answers we wish we had. We are perfect all the same.

Let's now focus on how you can live in your own personal high-heaven here on earth; level-shifting as you go, one manifestation at a time. This is how you 'hi-level' your life: you choose to see the beauty on the way. You look around one day and feel content. You smash an expensive Liberty teapot and you think, 'Ah well'. Your dog takes a shit on your new rug and you think, 'Hey ho, never mind, he's just a dog'. No matter what happens, you're OK. You're bouncing back anyway. And you didn't even need anything other than your fingertips to start accessing it. You're fully tapped in.

STOP OVERTHINKING AND START OVERFLOWING

When you're overthinking, you might find yourself stuck in what I call a 'negative selfing state': where self-doubt, self-sabotage, self-denial, self-suppression and self-effacement take the driving seat. It's where you turn inwards. And you get mean. Because, even more than taking a decent selfie, we love a good 'selfing'.

Selfing Applying focus on ourselves to deliver a negative or positive outcome (*my definition*)

We 'self' ourselves all the time, both negatively and positively. It's an ingrained pattern, constantly reinforced within our belief system – and that means it's addictive.

Like scrolling through selfies, looking for 'the one' worthy of posting (don't tell me you don't do that), we're wired to think about ourselves and present ourselves in a certain way. A very honest friend once told me I looked like a pouty fish in my selfies. I thought I looked like a sexpot. The problem was that I was so into my own selfie pose that I'd totally lost sight of another point of view. After this helpful advice (rude awakening), I started smiling more. Just like my unfortunate fish face, we can all get caught up in our own skewed opinion when it comes to what we say and think about ourselves. You might think you're bleugh, but someone else will think that you're a badass. You see, selfing can be brilliant if we are topping ourselves up with regular doses of self-belief, but dreadful if we have negative thought patterns on loop. If we learn our own unique set of 'selfing' beliefs we can get into the slipstream of a 'positive selfing state', where self-worth, self-belief, self-love and self-agency become our default vibe.

When we're tapped into a 'positive selfing state', we take back the power over how we respond to what happens in our reality. Rather than a reactive 'I hate my life', 'I doubt it' or 'I'm not good enough' mentality, swapping in positive selfing whilst tapping allows situations that seem like challenges (for example, being made redundant, a relationship breakdown, ending a toxic friendship, being in a job we hate, a change in financial circumstances) seem manageable or even exciting opportunities for positive growth, rather than opportunities to self-flagellate. I'm going to help you shift from negative selfing to positive selfing by the end of this journey, so help me god.

USE ME, BABY!

It's so important that you actually *practise* the techniques I will share with you. Tag me on Instagram when you see results, write all over this book, go back over things and be kind to yourself. If something is too much just come back to it another day. No one looks back on their life from their deathbed thinking, 'I wish I'd sent that extra email' – but we do, statistically speaking, regret passing up opportunities to have lived life authentically.

You can transform into the authentic you with consistent tapping. Taking just five minutes out of your day to swap an email for a self-expanding, results-giving and rapidly rewarding technique is so worth doing that I can't even fathom why you wouldn't.

Actually I can, remember: it's because you've been lied to. All through your early years and education you've been taught that you must work harder and push your body to the max to be productive, to compete with your friends at school for good grades, to do better, be better and not fail – to be *perfect* with your output, relationships and appearance. You are taught to be careful, avoid the unfamiliar and lower your expectations. You're taught to fit in, do what you're told and mistrust the new. We have been conditioned into a life of stress, and the very thought of making time to learn new, albeit simple and crucial, techniques like how to manage energy, how to stop hijacking our well-being ... well, that's just really low down on the to-do list. But slightly rejigging your to-do list in your favour can create massive gains.

LET'S TAP INTO MORE POSITIVE ENERGY

Start to notice *everything* is energy and that it's always on the move. Everything resonates. Even you. Don't think for a moment you are a solid, stuck thing: you're actually a magnificent malleable creature. You're pure energy. In Part Two we are really going to explore how this relates to your manifesting game. Because it *is* a game. It's fun to play with energetics. Energy can transform itself quick as a flash – just like ice turning to water, or water to steam. It's all the same *until it's commanded to change state*. Emotions are energy. You are energy. So powerfully command yourself to change state. Right now.

Let's get started.

THE KEY TAPPING POINTS – AND HOW TO TAP IN WITH ME

So where and how do we tap? I'll share the tapping points and various sequences that I've found most useful to me in terms of feeling happier, manifesting new possibilities and successful goal creation. EFT uses the meridian tapping points from Chinese medicine (similar to acupuncture) in a specific order with an emphasis on certain events, whereas I like to encourage a more intuitive, all-encompassing form of tapping. We will focus on the face points but will sometimes move beyond them to include the entire body, incorporate breathwork and movement, as well as introduce other energy-related, postural and neuro-linguistic techniques. If you've ever tapped with a practitioner before, you'll know that traditional EFT measures the intensity of an emotion as it decreases, while

I prefer to track the upward change in emotional *possibility* as it expands and increases usually as a percentage and through positive affirmations. Armed with tangible metrics, we tend to be more aware of our transformation, and focusing on a positive result is an important part of successful manifesting. Traditional EFT leans towards a 'search and destroy' pattern: pinpoint the memories that are holding you back and target the stress that they're causing you. I'll do some of this, but I also believe that you don't always need to be aware of the specific event that's causing you pain. Sometimes it's just a feeling you have and you can start with how your body feels. As we will discover, the body – as well as the mind – keeps the score.

The Rapid Tapping points form the basis for most of the tapping routines in this book. In this method, I encourage tapping on the face in one continuous flow, as it stimulates the ends of the meridian lines (balancing your energy flow) – and invigorates your facial muscles (reducing wrinkles as a happy bonus). When you tap, use both hands and tap for about ten seconds on each of the points with your fingertips. Using just your middle and index fingers is enough to do the job.

When you tap you should be gentle but firm, reserving a lighter touch for the under-eye area. Tired eyes can benefit from a light lymphatic touch, which increases blood flow to depuff your eye bags. I'm a big fan of skincare and feeling fresh – and there are cumulative beauty benefits that come with tapping daily – so I aim for my taps to be as close to an anti-ageing workout for your face as possible with elements of face yoga and massage incorporated to increase vitality, promote a youthful complexion, and even allow you to see a boost in your skin's collagen production. Think of these taps as like a HIIT class for your face *and* your emotional and mental well-being. Every time you tap in, you're toning your facial muscles, encouraging yourself to smile more and boosting your overall happiness.

Drawing on advice from doctors, I have also incorporated elements of psychodermatology, a cutting-edge discipline that draws a link between our skin health and our emotional health. While working in TV, I came up with the idea for a competition show about make-up for the BBC called *Glow Up*. On the surface it's about make-up artistry, but it's also about the value of authentic self-expression and acceptance. I want your taps to give *you* a glow up from the inside out – and since positive emotions can have a beneficial effect on the way we look it really is a win-win. You're welcome, send me all the flowers (and the before and after pics).

As Roald Dahl wrote in *The Twits*, a book my dad used to read to me:

'A person who has good thoughts cannot ever be ugly. You can have a wonky nose and a crooked mouth and a double chin and stick-out teeth, but if you have good thoughts they will shine out of your face like sunbeams and you will always look lovely.'

When you tap and manifest with me, I will also merge techniques such as body scanning, intention setting, future pacing, and laughter therapy, as well as 'shaking' the body to encourage positive free-flow of energy. In some taps, I will empower you to go freestyle and try intuitive tapping, where you choose your own points to tap on and move your body in accord with your new positive state.

When you're ready to seal in a high-vibrational energy we can say a True affirmation (we'll define these later) and you can administer more of a thumping motion on your chest (on your thymus gland – the part of you responsible for your immunity, and the 'happiness point' in tapping). I love ending a tap on this technique. Think Tarzan! It's so empowering! If you ever want to go deeper, visit www.rapidtapping.com for the most up-to-date way to access more routines and techniques.

As well as minimising stress, clearing away struggles and improving your skin health, I'll teach you how to use tapping to pave the way towards joyous manifestations of all kinds, such as:

- Sound sleep
- Dream lifestyle
- Super-solid self-belief
- Amazing love life
- Healthy immunity
- More money
- Unshakeable confidence
- More free time
- Big impact
- Ageless radiance
- Mind-blowing orgasms
- Like-minded friends
- Creative flow
- Massive productivity
- Unlimited abundance
- Crystal clarity

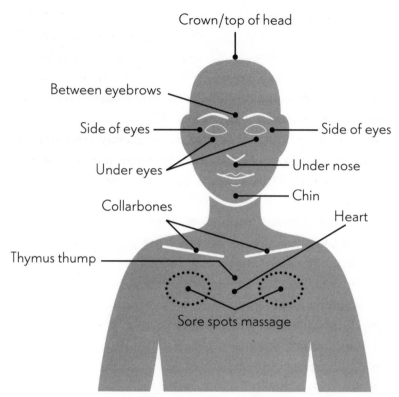

The Rapid Tapping points sequence

The Rapid Tapping points

- Sore spots massage
- Between eyebrows
- Side of eyes
- Under eyes (a lighter, fluttery pressure here)
- Under nose
- Chin

- Collarbones and heart area
- Crown/top of head

Additional points

Thymus thump Tarzan thump your upper chest with both fists. This is a quick way to activate your thymus gland, also called the 'happiness point' because it's linked to vitality, immunity and happiness. This energy technique is best known to neutralise negative energy and boost the immune system.

Finger tapping Using your thumbs, tap on the inner side of each finger in turn for about five seconds, over and over, with a light pressure. Perfect for when you need to keep your tapping discreet.

Head hug The head hug or head hold: hold one hand over your forehead and the other over the back of your head to soothe and seal in a calming energy.

MEASURING YOUR PROGRESS

Often it's enough to complete a tap and just notice the powerful shift in your energy or within your body, but I really like metrics. When you can see change, you can accept change. We directly measure the effectiveness in two key ways within Rapid Tapping:

Say it and score it By saying a positive affirmation out loud, tapping and then checking to see how much you believe it (giving it a score out of 100).

Using the frequency scale (-10 to +10) By noting your vibrational level on a scale, before and after a tap and also cumulatively over time (more on this in Chapter 5). The Frequency (Finder) Scale is a way to discover what your emotional feeling is at any given time. For example, imagine a sliding scale from -10 at the bottom (which is you feeling terrible) all the way up past 0 (which is just 'meh') towards +10 (where you feel joyful bliss).

Say it and score it

Begin by breathing and paying attention to your posture. State your positive affirmation aloud then score it out of 100 in terms of how believable it feels. You then check in throughout with the intention that your score *will* increase (it almost always does – but if it doesn't it's OK – just keep up the practice). Begin the tap with the clearing and releasing stage, then move onto the creating and manifesting stage. Once in a more positive state of mind, with energy flowing in a more shifted way and you feeling lighter, seal in the new vibration with some movement and repeat the affirmation to end the tap on a high.

The Rapid Tapping routine is as follows:

- SAY IT
- SCORE IT
- CLEAR IT
- CREATE IT
- SEAL IT
- SCORE IT

Sometimes it is useful to score it more often – and sometimes you'll find I skip a section – but in general this is the sequence to follow with the routines I am giving you.

THE SIGNATURE RAPID TAP

This is my go-to signature rapid tap which you can use every day, as many times as you like, to shift yourself into a more positive energy. It will take no more than a few minutes to feel the results.

Tapping exercise: Signature Rapid Tap

1   Inhale and exhale. Cross your arms in an X shape over your heart, with your palms placed above your collarbones.
2   Move your hands down and outwards a few inches from your collarbones to find what are known as the 'sore spots' (the name is pretty self-explanatory, as they should feel tender to touch) and massage with a medium pressure.
3   As you do so, repeat the following three steps out loud, filling in the blanks as you go:

I feel ...
Be honest – how do you feel? Try to give a name to the emotion. Whether good or bad, make sure to speak your truth. You can also preface this with: 'When I think about ... (e.g. your situation with your partner, your bank account, the day you've had). This additional step acknowledges the truth of your current reality.

Because ...
Ask yourself, why do you feel this way? This step gives voice to your current logical or emotional attachment.

And it's possible for me to . . .
Now it's time for you to add in a positive affirmation. It doesn't matter if it doesn't feel within reach yet, just give voice to your desire. This step focuses your tap on what you want to achieve (e.g. a brilliant relationship, a thriving career, true confidence).

SCORE IT Now score how possible and true this feels for you out of 100.

Think of it visually if you can; your intention is to raise your score by the end of the tap.

LIST IT Now make a list in your journal of all the reasons this *can't* be 100 per cent possible for you, to identify the blocks that stand in your way. You can write down any negative feelings about your potential, practical barriers or jot down any uncomfortable sensations in your body that you've noticed.

For example:
- I just can't do it
- I don't have enough confidence
- I have no experience in this area so it's not possible for me
- I can feel a weight on my shoulders
- I feel sick thinking about pushing myself again
- I'm not good enough.

CLEAR IT Now turn your focus to clearing the blocks by tapping through the Rapid Tapping points as you say each

one of your blocks out loud, allowing yourself to really
feel and *focus* as much as you can in the moment. If you
fully acknowledge and accept that your blocks exist in your
current reality, it will be easier to unhook yourself from the
negative energy attached to them from the past.

Inhale and exhale.

Make a note of how you feel. Do you feel calmer and
clearer already?

If you don't want to lose the new and improved energy
around what you want, start sealing it in. Remember: use it
or lose it!

SEAL IT It's time to notice the positive change occurring
and to seal that in like a glue. You'll do this by moving. Shake
your hands. Sing. Tap rapidly down your whole body to
wake it up. Wiggle or hum a tune. Engage your senses. Get
onboard with the way it feels in your body if you express
this feeling physically.

I feel ...
Notice and declare all the good feelings peeping through
you to seal them in. Tap through the Rapid Points as you
acknowledge each positive emotion or body response.

SAY IT **It is possible for me to ...**

Smile. State your affirmation again, out loud.

SCORE IT Now ask yourself how you feel. How possible does your affirmation feel out of 100? Smile, take a breath in through your nose and let it out through your mouth. You've just shifted energy and raised your vibration. Remember if it's even 1 per cent possible, it's not impossible. Keep breaking down the impossibility barrier! Keep tapping.

USING THE FLOW OF LIFE

Tapping can help you change beliefs by transforming negative thoughts and feelings, which you now know can change your energy. Once you've accessed a new frequency via tapping, you can take more positive steps towards your goals and move forward with confidence and ease. Let me introduce you to something I call the 'Flow of Life': a way to look at how your beliefs are made, reinforced and ultimately transformed.

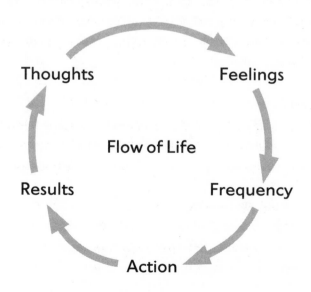

It all begins with your belief system, which is shaped via the unique circular flow shown in the illustration. Imagine that the outside edges of the circle are the constraints of your own belief system: the way you feel about yourself and the world. Your circle will expand as your belief system does, but will shrink if you ignore it. As your circle expands, more possibilities and opportunities open up. If you pay attention to the flow, from thoughts all the way to results, you can make big adjustments to what your reality looks like.

HACK: You may have read about the law of attraction, which teaches us that our thoughts create results – so if you think positively, over and over again, you will own a luxury yacht in three years' time. This isn't the whole story. Please remember: thinking happy thoughts about a yacht has nothing to do with owning a luxury yacht. Believing in your deepest core that you won't or shouldn't have one (because somewhere buried deep in your subconscious mind is a belief that all rich people are awful and you never want to be 'one of them') does do something. It blocks you from opening yourself up to the opportunity of owning one. Unconsciously, you'll create strategies to sabotage that reality.

The pivotal manifesting zone is your FREQUENCY – the vibrational level that you emit to other people and the Universe around you. Imagine you have a vibrational antenna which is either up or off. You're either the person others want to avoid in a room, or the one who attracts people like a bee to honey. From your FREQUENCY (vibration) you create a magnetic aura around you: just like a magnet, you can either attract or repel. You have a part to play in this: you take action either towards something or away from it. You bottle it, or you go for it. It depends on the energy of momentum behind it.

Once you have the ACTION steps in place, you can see a result and this becomes your reality. It will be on a sliding scale of positive or negative – what you want or what you don't want, and whether it's prompted by stress or a sense of calm. Caught up in all our actions is our own set of habits, behaviours and micro decisions. They flood in seconds before we make a move, just like a little mouse facing a cat and wondering whether to go left or right, anticipating an outcome. After ACTION comes tangible RESULTS. And when we see results, we believe something to be true.

So in order to get what we want in life, it's not *just* about action. In fact, we have all these different interception points in the flow of life. By scanning all the way back through the flow – from changing ACTIONS to assessing the FREQUENCY we emit, adjusting the FEELINGS that make up our emotional well-being, to understanding the everyday THOUGHTS that we have – we have a wealth of power to pivot into.

You are capable of expanding your possibilities because there are so many ways to adjust your beliefs.

2 SO WHAT DO YOU BELIEVE?

I'd like to use this chapter to show you how to adjust your beliefs using tapping, so that they're less limiting and more helpful. Limiting beliefs create stress and, as we know, stress not only makes us feel terrible but can also leave our skin visibly inflamed and haggard. However, tapping consistently on these beliefs can help thwart your negative cycle – it's time to shift your perspective.

When you have a belief, you take it as given that that's the way things are. After a while, you unconsciously come up with strategies to prove your belief to be true; none of us like having our beliefs challenged. Can you see how negative beliefs about yourself and the world start to hold you back? Do any of these feel familiar to you?

- I'm not perfect
- I don't belong
- I'm unworthy
- I'm unlovable

When we ignore the limiting beliefs at the core of our being, we open ourselves up to a cycle of self-blame. So when you have your vision and goals, it's so important to address your core beliefs rather than just your actions or your habits.

HOW BELIEFS HELP US MANIFEST

The woman who manifested the love of her life? She believed she was worthy. Her belief system matched her envisioned life. This is because she started taking strategic action that felt inspired and adopted slight modifications to her behaviours that propelled her towards her positive outcome. She didn't use dating apps, try to play a numbers game or compromise on what she wanted in a partner. She concentrated on emitting a certain frequency of loving empowerment, even when it seemed very unlikely that the right person was on the horizon. She chose to love each person as she would want to be loved in return, and tapped on past guilt and blame as it came up from various triggers. She focused on believing that she was attuned for success. This woman was me. Can you hope or think your way into this energetic frequency? No. Does having some negative thoughts about achieving a loving relationship mean we manifest a negative one? No. We cannot control our thoughts and we must not be afraid of ourselves. But can you tap your way to another frequency? Another vibration of energy? *Absolutely*. And does that bring you real results? Hell yes.

We don't manifest from our thoughts alone but from the energy vibration we emit, which others can sense. This energy is inextricably linked to our unique belief system. Our actions are motivated by our feelings, and when our actions come from an energy that eventually shouts, 'Yes, this is believable and possible', we see the results that we're looking for. This in turn creates a circular loop of healthier, happier thoughts, which will allow us to manifest more effectively and rapidly.

> **HACK:** Consistent tapping transforms your energetic system so that you can become more open and positive. This will take time and dedication, but the more you tap, the more you will be able to manifest at speed because your frequency will become like an open channel in the vast seas of possible destinations. There will be no warships blocking your way. You will become electric, magnetic even. This is because you can only receive from the universe what you perceive to be available for you.

I'll never forget the time I manifested exactly £1700, when on the very same day £1700 left my bank account because of an unexpected membership renewal. I wanted to buy my son a car and focused on receiving the exact sum I wanted – £3500 – and that took just three days to pop up in the form of an unexpected bonus.

Am I special? No. Am I a witch? No. Was it a flukey coincidence? No! Did I *believe* it was fully possible for me to receive the exact sum of money into my bank account in such a short time? Yes. If you can rapidly create results in one area of your life you can do it in all areas – provided you adjust your belief system so that it feels extremely possible in each area. That's what my entire Rapid Tapping method is based on: tangible results achieved by raising your self-belief that you are able to live the life (and lifestyle) you desire.

Wand or weapon?

Your belief about something can be a wondrous magic wand or a weapon of mass destruction – it's up to you. The more you repeat a belief, the more it will make sense and encourage you to take meaningful action in your life. Your brain is creating new neural pathways all the time based on what you believe to be true at any given moment: you are not stuck where you are. You may just be repeating the same unhelpful beliefs, which are possible to change.

Many of our ingrained beliefs are negative. We are led and sustained by this set of core beliefs (of which we may be unaware) that impact every part of our life by way of our behaviours, potential and actions. Core beliefs run deep, and you may have experienced their effects before but been unable to recognise the root cause. Maybe you keep having failed relationships, but can't understand why. You've spoken to a therapist for five years about a trauma but you're still carrying the root cause in your frequency. Or perhaps you've acknowledged the existence of these negative or limiting beliefs, but you're unsure about how to get rid of them. You know that acknowledging a belief doesn't make it go away ... so what does? We'll learn how to do this step by step in my 'clear to create' approach, so that you can get on with living a life of freedom. Remember:

> *Your beliefs about a result must match the frequency of the outcome you want in order for you to create it and then sustain it.*

WHAT DO YOU REALLY BELIEVE IN?

Tapping exercise: The Believability Factor

It's time to establish your core positive belief capacity. I use this exercise a lot with my clients, and it's a useful one to revisit too.

Let's start deep and go straight to the positive core belief statements (I've really struggled with some of these myself, so don't worry if you start off with very low scores). Gently remind yourself that it's not impossible to raise your scores. To begin transforming your beliefs, make sure you've got a journal and pen to hand. This can sometimes be uncomfortable, difficult work so make sure you have tissues close by in case you're confronted with anything that needs to be cleared. And remember to be compassionate to yourself – you are amazing.

Say these core belief statements one by one out loud to yourself, noticing how believable each one feels to you. Then rank each statement on a scale of 0 to 100: 100 means it's so damn believable, it's basically happened, while 0 means it couldn't be farther away from being a reality.

- I am wonderful
- I can create money easily
- I am always enough
- I am happy and content

- I am empowered
- I am in charge of my own life
- I am beautiful
- I am productive
- I live in a kind universe
- I am a master manifestor
- I can direct my own life
- I take full responsibility for my own well-being
- I am worthy beyond measure
- I am fully and unconditionally lovable
- It is safe to love and be loved
- I belong here.

The closer we can align ourselves to these positive beliefs, the more we can see and accept possibilities and opportunities.

So how did you score? I've had clients come to me with a mixed bag ranging from 10 per cent to 80 per cent, depending on the statement. It doesn't matter what your pre-tap score is. Over time, with consistent tapping, you'll raise your pre-tap percentages on each core belief. If you practise this exercise regularly for over a year, you should see your percentages go up and up and up.

Which statements scored lowest on the percentage scale? Usually, the lower the score, the more the belief has been recycled, because your brain is so familiar with your response and the energy behind it is strong. At first this may seem like an epic, impossible task. And I won't lie to you: we need discipline to adjust core beliefs.

Your brain doesn't want you to change your beliefs

You will need to call upon your willpower when you want to change a belief. It's not as easy as we would like, and here's why. Scans (EEGs) that measure activity in the brain indicate that when our beliefs are challenged, our brain responds in the way it would if we were running for our lives. We get defensive and stressed. If we want change we need to learn to sit with this unique tension and not give up too quickly, as it's part of the process.

In one study conducted by the University of Southern California's Brain and Creativity Institute, assistant research professor of psychology Jonas Kaplan asked participants provocative questions relating to their political beliefs, and then monitored their brain activity. The study revealed that when our beliefs are directly challenged by new information, areas of our brain that are usually alert when we experience physical threats begin to show increased activity. So our minds aren't exactly primed to change these core beliefs; quite the opposite, in fact, because we resist change on a neurological level.

Your brain's ability to react in this way is linked to its emotional response centre. This is also why we have phobias. After being bitten by a dog, for years I believed that all dogs wanted to bite me. Whenever I tried to be brave and pretend that I wasn't scared by a small dog, I would fake it by telling myself that the dog was cute and fluffy – but my brain was prepping me for full-on panic. I'd be caught in a familiar and repetitive pattern of sweating, shaking, seizing up or running away – typical fight-or-flight reactions – the energetic and emotional attachments stored within me when I was bitten as a child were also being reinforced. Initially that emotional attachment was betrayal, as the six-year-old processed this as 'How could my best friend bite me?'

Now, after many futile years of trying to talk myself out of my fear and feeling useless due to my brain's automatic response, I've finally managed to overcome my phobia with tapping. I'm even the proud owner of a gorgeous Cavapoo who is my dearest BFF. I've also become more compassionate towards myself because I understand where the fear came from and why it was so hard to shift. It wasn't just an irrational fear, the feeling of betrayal was so strong that my fear of dogs was a *belief response*. I believed any dog would bite me and my wonderful brain was protecting me by remembering a reaction that might just keep me safe – flushing my body with adrenalin, cortisol and fight-or-flight chemicals to keep me away from the very devil himself, Fido. Growl.

KNOWING YOUR MANIFESTATION BASELINE

Once you become determined to start raising the percentage of one of your core beliefs, you'll soon notice how your overall frequency starts to rise up too. What I call your 'baseline' in Rapid Tapping is a trackable indicator of your mindset, your emotions and your manifestations. Our aim here is to create a higher percentage of validity on the positive beliefs you have about yourself and the world. But if you feel like you're holding back and finding it difficult to adopt a more positive 'hi-life' outlook, try tapping on the negative narrative that's blocking you from feeling like you can have a 100 per cent life in all areas. Remember, all we have is now. Our current reality isn't wrong. The meaning we attach to it is what counts; change the story.

Tapping exercise: The Negative Narrative Tap

SAY IT **I am able to have a 100 per cent life in *all* areas.**
Say this affirmation out loud.

SCORE IT How believable is that affirmation to you right now, out of 100? Be honest.

CLEAR IT Sore spots massage:

When I think about having a 100 per cent life in all areas:

- I feel some blocks around it
- How is it even possible?
- All areas?
- It feels out of reach
- I'm being shy about my life
- I can feel this in my body right now (sense and scan your body for clues: what can you notice?)
- Yes, I can feel this
- It's not fully possible for me yet
- Maybe because I've seen some old evidence in my life
- Or the lives of others
- That makes me feel like I am not able to have a 100 per cent life
- This is just my current belief about what is possible
- And that's OK
- But I now choose to change that viewpoint
- I am actually quite able to use tapping now
- I have a tool that can help me eliminate negative beliefs

- This is a very good position to be in!
- I am grateful for this
- I am ready to start now and change my story
- I am ready to tap in more each day
- This can feel more possible for me.

If you check your score at this point, and you're feeling that the affirmation is already much more possible (for example, 75 per cent) you may wish to stop. But if you have time (and you do!) head to the next section, where you tap through the rapid points with the positive intention of releasing.

Move through the Rapid Tapping points as you say the following script:

- I have all these lingering doubts about how possible this is
- Who am I to have it all?
- I don't really deserve to have everything, do I?
- I haven't always been able to love myself deeply and totally
- So maybe I should just stick to having a few good areas of my life
- Other people struggle, actually
- So isn't it bad that I could be happy in all parts of my life?
- I do want to open up to new possibilities
- But what will change if I do?
- Lots of things might change
- Who will I become if I make these changes in my life?
- I know that changing my beliefs is scary for my brain
- Maybe I won't even recognise myself?
- Maybe I would change my family dynamic?

- Or my friends would change?
- Or maybe these are just my fears of the unknown
- Maybe I would just be happier!
- So I decide right now to make these positive changes and trust
- I want to change my beliefs about myself
- I am not feeling hugely confident about it all yet
- But I am willing to see where this leads me
- I know it's at least 1 per cent possible.

SCORE IT Check in with yourself by saying the affirmation again:
I am able to have a 100 per cent life in *all* areas.

How possible is it out of 100 now? Score gone up? If yes, keep going ... if not, keep tapping through the clearing script and allow your intuition to guide you into other aspects that are holding you back from truly believing the positive affirmation.

CREATE IT Tap through these relevant positive affirmations as you move through the Rapid Tapping points.

- I actually CAN up-level my life
- I am noticing that this feels a bit more possible than it did before
- My life is important to me
- I am ready to do this
- I am empowered by this
- I am free to do this!
- I can do it

- I am intuitive
- I trust life is bringing me to my highest good
  and potential
- My energy is changing
- I'm capable and focused
- I can feel this in my body
- I am ready to receive now
- I know it's possible.

SEAL IT Now, what do you notice? Usually you'll feel more
positive now. Once your energy is on the move and you are
feeling a bit of a shift then you can seal it in, by mindfully
allowing this energy to connect and calibrate your belief
system. Let your unconscious do its job and upgrade
your operating system for you. Remember, you can't get
this wrong!

Move your body, dance or smile to get your body into this
belief as well as your mind. Say the affirmations that struck a
chord with you, repeating them with more of a rapid energy,
getting some momentum going as you tap through the points.

Freestyle with the points you feel most intuitively led to
tap, for example:

I am ready to do this!
I am free to do this!

AFFIRM IT Thump your thymus three times with intention
and conviction while repeating:

I am able to have a 100 per cent life in all areas
I am able to have a 100 per cent life in all areas
I am able to have a 100 per cent life in all areas
It is possible for me.

Do things feel more possible? What's your score out of 100 now? This is just the beginning of where tapping can take you. Buckle up!

STOP TRYING TO CONTROL YOUR THOUGHTS

Your brain can process eleven million pieces of information every second, but your conscious mind can only get to grips with forty to fifty pieces. Trying to catch one is like trying to catch a hundred chickens at once. It won't work. Even trying to catch one chicken is incredibly annoying. Stop trying to catch and control your thoughts – even those negative ones.

EFT is all based around the negatives, and you need them in order for tapping to work well at clearing blocks. Negative thoughts, limiting beliefs and inner gremlins are not just welcomed but essential. Phew! Give yourself a nice pat on the back for being a human and knowing that our mind isn't capable of being in a positive mode all day long. Let yourself off the hook.

What you can concern yourself with is how *dominantly* those thoughts come to you and if you dwell on them. What is the energy you give them? The more you focus on something, the more energy there is behind it. The more you dwell on a thought, the more it becomes an emotionally charged feeling. As you do so, your brain will create a stronger neural pathway to this thought, paving the way for it to become a core belief. We then see and perceive everything around us through this unique filter of beliefs. This can be fabulous if you've been reinforcing positive beliefs over and over again – or a shit show if you've experienced, like most of us, all kinds of big and small traumas, bad experiences or toxic people. You're in a loop one way or the other and the flow of life is either for you or against you – so what do you choose?

If you choose to create results that you love, you're going to need to focus on the energy from now on, not the thoughts alone. Remember The Flow of Life? It's your energy *frequency* that matters, and I'm going to demystify that for you right now.

ENERGY – NOT YOU – CREATES RESULTS

In my world of teaching the art and science of creating wild, wonderful results, there's a simple rule:

> *If your energy doesn't match the energy of the result you want, your result is not going to be easy to bring into reality. Instead you will feel like you're pushing.*

You expend huge amounts of energy if you tend to force success by determination alone. And worse, all of that pushing may make you burn out in the process of trying to make stuff happen.

There's a better way than pushing and wading through the mud of our past to get to the other side. If someone else has remastered a belief about themselves why can't you? Use me as an example here. I used to truly believe:

- I am unattractive – nobody wants me.
- I am incapable – I'm not good enough.

- I am trapped – I can't change.
- I am unworthy of a wonderful partner – if I have a good relationship, my work will suffer.
- I am always abandoned – they will leave me.
- I am an outsider – I don't belong – I'm different.
- I am too much – I stand out. Keep quiet.

When I say these now I laugh out loud, because I recognise that they're absolutely untrue. I used to carry these beliefs around with me in two ways – aware and unaware – and you're most likely the same. We don't always *know* we have a belief. We are unaware. We're not conscious of it. We need to dig around to find it. Practices like therapy, CBT and hypnotherapy really help us become more aware.

Take my quashed false belief around my appearance.

'I am unattractive'

Ouch. Yes. This is a belief that crippled me, very consciously, for years. I had freckles back in the day when every freckle was rigorously airbrushed out of conversation, let alone on the models in the magazines. In my mind, I was a reject. I was also a late developer, had inherited a fat neck off my dad (cheers), and went to an all-girls school where I was devoid of even the most desperate boy's attention . . . and I believed 100 per cent that I was unattractive.

Years went on and I reinforced this belief. In a practical way, I didn't ask out any boys who were considered 'hot'. When, sweating with fear, I finally called up a boy I fancied, who was broadly considered 'hot', to ask him out, his response was 'I like you as a friend.' It was a dagger through the heart and another notch on my 'unattractive' belief bedpost of lies.

With lifelong mindset work, some positive experiences out-weighing the negative ones and a determination to reframe this, I made progress. What accelerated it all was tapping: I now believe I am attractive and I love my freckles. Better still, I ask out the hot boys and know I deserve a wonderful man who inspires me because I believe I am attractive inside and out, even with C-section scars, wrinkles and whatever. I am energetically aligned to my worth and am full of self-love. But the point I'm making here is that this was an *aware* core belief.

There are also beliefs that are hidden away, latent, sneaky. Like the goblin in the forest blocking you at every turn, *unaware* core beliefs exist too. These are the ones you just don't register, that you might not even consciously *think* you believe. But still, deep down, in your energetic coding, they're true. Your mind will unconsciously try to prove these ingrained beliefs in everything you do because they're familiar and that's how we are designed. Remember your brain hates belief change? It might sound twisted but, neurologically speaking, we do attempt to prove ourselves right, even when the belief makes no logical sense to someone else. Confirmation bias is the way we embrace information that supports our beliefs and reject any information that contradicts them.

If something is a core belief, we are hardwired to see it everywhere. For example, take the idea of being unattractive. If someone in a coffee shop so much as glances at you when you order full-fat milk, your brain may automatically respond with, 'They're telling me I'm a fat, unattractive mess.' No, that's not true.

You see, beliefs are all about perception. What you believe can be totally obvious to you or really hidden away, but sabotaging you just as much as the beliefs you are consciously aware of.

Here's another one I had for years that unknowingly affected all my relationships. Maybe you can relate to it in some way?

'I am always abandoned'

It's not really something that you want to bring up at the dinner table, is it. I won't be sipping this one out over a bottle of Rioja with Ted and Lucy. But nonetheless, I dug it out as something I could acknowledge and work with.

I was working with a skilled EFT practitioner and healer who led me back through my life to my inner child and a memory of my dad being diagnosed with cancer and my fear that he would die. Then I went through the timeline of my life to another memory, where more and more people disappeared. And then my dad died. And then my grandma died. And then it just became so ingrained that *subconsciously* I started to welcome that abandonment. It was what I was familiar with and it made sense to me on some profound level. I believed that I was someone who would be abandoned.

I'll be very upfront now as I think my own healing around this will support yours. This led to a string of strange relationships, where I thought I was anxious AF and was constantly worried my partner would leave me. This was compounded when my marriage fell apart. In recent years, however, I've realised that – shock horror – I was the avoidant one after all, because I was picking people who – on some deep level – I knew it wouldn't work out with in the end. Then as each relationship came to a close, perhaps in some masochistic way I could go, 'Oh look, abandoned again!' Then my core belief would become further entrenched. Even if I called things off I would still see myself as abandoned, because they didn't go the distance and chase me or change for me.

I realised this was *my* issue (after all, I'm the common denominator) and taking 100 per cent responsibility gave me back my freedom and power. What part of your life do you really want to change? Your beliefs will guide you or grind against you. So when I finally dealt with my own Achilles' heel, I became free from this debilitating and totally untrue belief that felt like a fact. I rearranged that BS and turned that negative core belief into a positive story of true self-worth.

Self-worth is something that the majority of my clients need to work on, and it's at the heart of all manifestation work. In order to fully believe something is possible you need to know that you are worthy of it. And that requires super self-worth! I have a tap for you on this now. This can be repeated as many times as you like – and remember you are worthy. No matter what.

SELF-WORTH: SKYROCKET YOUR MANIFESTING POWER

Many of us believe that our self-worth is conditional, and that we are only worthy if we fulfil an arbitrary list of impossible require-ments that we set ourselves. As a society, somewhere along the line we've developed a toxic co-dependent relationship with results. Our sense of self is bound up in external determinants.

Do any of these self-worth determinants resonate with you?

- My worth depends on how much money I have.
- My worth depends on what people think about me.
- My worth depends on being successful.
- My worth depends on my career.

I could go on . . . could you?

What our early caregivers thought of our potential, the patterns of previous relationships and how we've been socially conditioned to experience life all contribute to the story of our self-worth. Let me ask you this: what does it mean to you to be worthy of what you want? What are your 'worth criteria'? Journal these right now – make a list of five things that make you feel a sense of worth. Then ask yourself: what would have to happen externally in your life to make you feel unworthy?

When I teach people to manifest using tapping it's really about being totally at peace with the present moment, the present you and the presence by which you navigate life. If you have that, you have it all. It's not wrong to want beautiful things for yourself, but you don't need any luxury trappings to be enough. Let that be your first intention each day: you are *enough*, exactly as you are. Even if you experience feelings of guilt, shame or suffer from imposter syndrome – whatever it is – it doesn't make you any less worthy, ever. Bringing these emotions to the surface with tapping shows that you're human, and that we are a collection of our experiences, endeavours and traumas. With every tap, a new gremlin might pop up that makes us feel unworthy again. Ditch that! You are worthy. Worthy to live your dreams. Worthy to take action. To let it all happen.

And if you feel a greater sense of unconditional self-worth after this tap, that's an important step towards manifesting the life you want. Repeat to reinforce that belief. Over and over. We manifest from a state of being, which really must be from a place of worthiness.

Begin by taking full responsibility for your own well-being.

Tapping exercise: The Self-worth Core Routine

1 Have a sip of water, because this is energy work and it's most efficient when we are hydrated. Now make yourself comfortable, sitting or standing, and relax into yourself. Notice your posture, straighten your spine.

2 How are you feeling? Focus on the connection of your body to your surroundings, the soles of your feet to the ground. Bring intention to that right now, and feel the scan of intention going up through your feet, up through your body until you come to your heart. Place your hands over your heart and let that intention run up over your head and fall like a beautiful, gorgeous light that is guiding you.

3 Take a deep breath in through your nose and exhale consciously through your mouth – perhaps connecting to a particular scent, one that you can make ritualistic each time you use this self-worth tap.

SAY IT **'I am worthy'**.
Say this affirmation out loud.

Notice how true this statement feels to you on a scale of 1 to 100.

Now take a moment to acknowledge yourself on a BIG level, and say 'I am part of the universe'. This kind of 'super worth' means that we are all sublimely worthy in all capacities: we deserve to have our needs met in every aspect of our lives, to have our values respected and to have a non-negotiable attitude to anything that makes us feel powerless, 'less than', shameful, guilty or not enough in any way. We deserve this simply by existing! So knowing that, let's say again: **'I am worthy'**.

SCORE IT What's your current percentage?

Be honest with yourself here. Saying an affirmation out loud and thinking, 'Yeah, I would like to be worthy', is totally different from the reality of how it actually *feels* and sits in the body. This may be uncomfortable for you; confronting, even. So take yourself to a time in your life where you have not felt worthy, you have not felt enough. Don't wonder about why, don't analyse it, just remind yourself of it now – go for the most powerful one, because the earliest and most potent memory will be the most effective. If you repeat this tap, you simply work through memories, beginning with the most intense.

Tune in to that negative emotional attachment and close your eyes. Take yourself into that place, which may feel negative, it may feel emotional. That's OK. The aim with tapping is to trigger the patterned responses so that we can start to work with them. Allow yourself to be in that memory. Now it's time to say that affirmation out loud, one more time: **'I am worthy'**.

Not many of you will have started at 100 per cent, because life happens and patterns set in, habits form, patterns are reinforced.

CLEAR IT Sore spots massage: move your hands to the sore spots. Massage both spots as you acknowledge the truth of how you feel:
'Even though I do not feel fully worthy, I choose to love and accept myself anyway. Even though I do not feel fully worthy because ...'

List some reasons and feelings why you don't feel worthy. Unless you're at 100 per cent believable level when you say this aloud, you can accept, for now, that you feel unworthy.

Now do your three-step routine, filling in the blanks with your own words:

I feel unworthy
Because ...
But I choose to love and accept myself anyway.

Tap through the Rapid Tapping points, starting with 'between eyebrows':
I don't feel worthy enough.

Move on to the next tapping point in the sequence with each new statement – you can also use your own words at any point:

- I do not feel worthy enough and I really wish that I did, actually.
- Why don't I feel worthy enough? Maybe it's because ...

Really start to unpick what might come up for you intuitively here:

- Maybe it's because ...
- Or maybe because ...
- and all these things that have happened to me and all these things that I've done
- Somehow make me feel not enough
- And it also makes me feel ...
- And I feel emotional about it actually
- I feel ...
- I just don't feel that I have the self-worth I want yet
- I am not 100 per cent
- Will I ever be?
- It is possible, perhaps
- Maybe I don't believe in myself enough
- Maybe I don't fully love myself enough
- Maybe because ...
- And it plays on my mind sometimes
- It affects the decisions I make
- It holds me back
- It stops me from living in my dreams and it stops me from achieving my goals
- It even stops me from setting goals
- Will I ever even be enough, ever?
- I formed a belief once
- Probably when I was little
- A belief about myself and what I was worth
- Maybe I remember why I thought that
- I'll think about it now
- Maybe as an adult I remember that stuff
- Or my brain remembers that stuff for me
- And my energy is stuck around it

- I have experienced things in my life that have made this feel like fact
- But it isn't factually correct
- And I don't want to have that story running my life any more.

CREATE IT Continue to tap through the Rapid Tapping points:

- So I powerfully decide to accept that I am more worthy than I thought I was
- Every tap that I take is changing things a little bit, maybe changing my beliefs about myself
- Maybe changing beliefs about the world
- I can control how kind I am to myself
- What if I was kinder to myself, starting NOW?
- What if I saw myself as that little version of me, a child
- And I just gave that little me some extra love
- How would that feel for me?
- If I loved the little me
- I give love to that little me inside.

1 Place your hands over your heart and close your eyes, taking deep breaths in through your nose. Exhale and allow your breath to just be exactly as it needs to be right now. Sit in silence for a moment visualising the little you.

2 Take yourself back to you as a child, maybe seeing yourself with compassion. Ask that little you if there's anything they needed to hear or have back then – maybe a message, maybe just a cuddle, to be heard, or some love. See the innocence in the eyes of the younger you. Perhaps before something was taken away or changed.

3 Keeping your eyes closed, bring your hands into a tap on your collarbones and heart area. Imagine that you are tapping for the little you, bringing the emotions that they once felt to the surface to be dealt with, cleared and healed.

4 Allow any energy that has been stuck for so long to shift and start to move again. Ever so slowly visualise the energy as a little ball of light that's spreading out and taking its natural form, before it goes out through your body and into the atmosphere again.

5 Tap gently on your collarbones. With every tap you are helping to heal and provide love for the little you, that then shifts into the you right now. It is possible for you to have a natural, harmonious feeling of worth coming through your body because you are worthy ... so say it with me now, again: '**I am worthy**'. As you say it, you know on a deep level that you are indeed worthy, even if it doesn't feel like it 100 per cent right now. We can choose to lean on the feelings of love, compassion, kindness and worth. And if you feel that you can do that, very gently open your eyes and then continue to tap while you say,
   I choose to feel compassionate and kind to myself right now.

6 Allow yourself to really feel what it means to be kind and compassionate to yourself. Allow everything in the moment to pass through. Everything is transient and moving. Any energy that has been stuck for so long is passing through again, like the stagnant river, moving once more. And as you tap, you'll feel more connected to the little you and the you now and the you of the future.

7 Hold your heart and allow yourself to sigh or breathe as you like. Just allow any release and shift and change to happen. Don't fight it, let it pass, and allow yourself to be in the moment.

SCORE IT Notice how believable that feels again as a percentage.

AFFIRM IT Say out loud the affirmation statement: '**I am worthy**'.

Now when you say that, notice a shift and seal it in by acknowledging it. Does this affirmation now feel more believable than when you started the tap? If it feels a little (or a lot) more believable, then accept it as a fact. Woohoo! A new neural pathway is now in place. Now, without worrying about any points, tap along your whole body to embrace this new belief. Remember, clearing limiting beliefs and sealing in the new frequency is such a big part of manifestation tapping.

In the unlikely event that the statement doesn't feel more believable, you can continue to clear by tapping through the points and repeating:

- I choose to know that I can feel worthy
- Maybe it is OK for me to feel enough?
- I give myself permission to be enough
- What if I don't need to do anything to prove that?
- Even though I might have felt in the past that I do need to prove my worth
- And I might still feel like that now

- I choose to know that there is a possibility that I could step into my true worth
- Maybe the healing won't start now but perhaps it will tomorrow
- I choose to know that on some level I am so worthy of my desires
- I choose to know this, I choose to remember every day that I can love myself unconditionally
- No matter what happens around me, or how I react to that, I am always worthy
- I am always enough.

Keep repeating this exercise, because different aspects that block us from coming into our super self-worth will dissolve with each tap. Draw on your senses as you tap, because what you feel or smell or hear can help us connect to positive energy and make space for us to manifest. Knowing that we can connect back through our own personal timeline to our inner child is really powerful. The relief of tapping into the emotions behind the younger version of ourselves is a deep healer.

Take a moment to recalibrate. Think about how your answers to questions about your self-worth have changed — it might be only a slight change, or the shift might feel profound.

JOURNAL IT Without thinking about it too much, write about what happened during your tapping experience.

Once you've done that, answer these journal prompts honestly:

What positive results would I see if I gave myself full permission to be worthy?

What have I been holding onto that I am willing to let go of for my own benefit?

Truly, what possibilities would open up for me if I woke up each morning and tapped?

What beliefs did I once hold that no longer have the same power over me?

Repeating this self-worth tap regularly, perhaps weekly as a self-care ritual, is going to help you shift into a state of possibility and opportunity, love and contentment over time. One of my clients repeated this tap over fifty times to massive effect. Each time she tapped she found a new way to love herself, because each practice unfolded slightly differently, allowing her to experience a lot of a-ha moments. If we don't repeat, we are less likely to be aware of our own patterns and how can we break free from a negative cycle when we're not conscious of it to begin with? Repetition will help you reduce any feelings of unworthiness so you can slip into a flow state with less subconscious or energetic resistance.

HACK: You're only fully able to access your own flow if you commit to your own inner connection and continue this work diligently with self-compassion and excitement for what is possible if you do.

EMBRACING NEW BELIEFS REQUIRES FAITH AND IMAGINATION

We don't tend to perceive something for what it is until we see it up close and personal. In your life, if you've seen something as real, you have faith in it. But can we believe in something *before* it even exists for us?

We know we can 100 per cent achieve what we have previously done or perceived as possible, but a level of faith is needed when we embrace changes in our belief system.

Katie, a theatre fundraiser and actress who has used my manifesting process, is someone who resolutely decided to embrace transformation, even though she didn't know what was waiting for her:

> I had no idea what I was going to get from this process when I started this life-changing course except a pull to discover more. The progress literally creeps up on you and suddenly I had clarity that I hadn't expected.
>
> Now, I make firm decisions, where I used to wobble or listen to someone else's opinion before going ahead with something. I'm resolute. I'm ambitious without fearing failure, seeing it more as a life experience. All the things we're taught to fear or accept are no more for me and I look forward to creating the next thing.

'By believing passionately in something that still does not exist, we create it. The non-existent is whatever we have not sufficiently desired.'

FRANZ KAFKA, novelist

Think about what you want for a minute. Even though your dreams don't exist in your reality yet, sufficient focus, faith and action – together with the techniques coming up – *can* help you create them.

Knowing the limits of 'human energy'

When you actively pursue a desire of the heart, action can be exhausting and willpower limited; studies show that you're full of willpower in the mornings but that it dwindles during the day. And when you operate on willpower alone, you're giving yourself two possible realities: if I do this, I'm strong; if I fail, I'm weak. Willpower is the springboard for the creative cycle, but it cannot sustain you for the entire ride. If you insist on trying to achieve through relying on your will alone, you'll end up navigating life on your reserve tanks, which is something I call 'human energy'. This kind of energy is finite, but in practising Rapid Tapping we can kickstart and rebalance our body by releasing the happy hormones of serotonin, dopamine and oxytocin. It's like going to the gym knackered and feeling great when you come out. It's chemical.

Universal Energy is infinite; we just need to remember that its flow and balance can get blocked up, and that we have the power to move stuck energy. Remember that energy can transmute – or change form – easily: so ice can turn into water and that can turn into steam. Perhaps you're stuck in the emotional equivalent of ice? Universal Energy never runs out, it just requires faith in its existence – so why do we persist in operating solely on human energy, which is finite?

Tapping exercise: Tapping out your Impossibility Factors

Let's do a very quick exercise on the impossibility factors separating you from your desires.

1   Write down one big life desire that feels much less than 100 per cent possible to you right now. Like a lofty promotion, a dream home, a soulmate, or an unshakeable feeling of peace.
2   Write a list of five 'Impossibility Factors' that have convinced you that it's more impossible than possible. You're looking for any barriers between you and your envisioned, fulfilled life. These can be beliefs, assumptions or practical factors.
3   Now, identify the evidence that proves this. You're looking for reasons *why* it's impossible based on your perceptions. People, experiences, movies, caregivers: discover where this might have come from. This is your current proof (not verified, universal fact).
4   Go back through each piece of 'proof' and tap on your collarbones and heart area as you disprove and debunk each piece of inconclusive evidence. You do this by using the following script.

Tapping on your collarbones and heart:

• When I think about my desire to . . . (add your desire)
• I have inconclusive evidence that . . . (add your 'proof')
• But I refuse to believe this from now on

- Because it is not true for everyone
- Therefore it is not 100 per cent fact for me
- Which means it is not impossible
- Which means it's possible
- My desire is possible.

Repeat this for each piece of evidence you have identified. Debunk those impossibilities one by one and squash them like a bunch of grapes. Your limiting beliefs are not made of cast iron, they're like squishy fruit. Squish 'em.

3 ACKNOWLEDGING THE POWER OF YOUR MIND

This chapter is all about acknowledging the power of the mind, how to access your hidden potential and gaining a real understanding of what role the energy of possibility plays in the quest for our ultimate life.

To start understanding the science behind tapping, I need to take you back to a period of great heartache in my life. As a little girl, I first learned about the power of the mind from my dad, a self-made man whose entrepreneurial energy enabled my parents to own their house outright in their early twenties. My parents had a happy marriage and thriving careers, and even though they both experienced humble upbringings, they really pushed themselves to get where they wanted to be. For quite a few years everything in their lives was golden.

However, that is not the story I want to tell. Stress and striving for success were not, as it happens, his friends. When he was just thirty my dad had a heart attack. I vaguely remember my panic at the time; even at such a young age, I knew that a heart attack wasn't good. Turns out it was worse. It was actually a tumour wrapped around his heart, which had stopped it from beating.

Within days he was diagnosed with a highly advanced and rare adrenal cancer that had already spread to his lungs. It was incurable, and despite a mammoth eight-hour keyhole surgery, he was given ten days to live.

But that wasn't the end – what happened after the diagnosis was incredible. It's the reason I do what I do and the passionate energy behind all the words in this book. Refusing to be knocked back by the awful news, my dad focused on living fully in the moment and adopting a positive mindset. With support from my mum, he managed to pass the ten-day prognosis – it was a miracle. Soon, he was slowly back on his feet. He continued to surprise his doctors at each medical assessment. Year after year he continued to thrive. I barely ever saw him without a smile on his face and yet after the diagnosis my parents were no longer able to run their businesses and narrowly escaped bankruptcy. They lost it all, but gained everything.

My dad rejected stress. His strategy was to focus purely on altruism, giving back and being kind. He began working with the homeless as a local councillor to activate social change. He had a number of creative passions, from painting and journalling to meditating and praying. He studied the power of energetics each day, using his mind as fiercely and diligently as a monk. He manifested like a pro and his emotional well-being was off the charts, despite the health diagnosis on paper. He had so much human energy and genuine optimism – he told me anything was possible in life and I believed him.

I've come to realise that my dad was truly happy, despite the pain he had to endure each day. With his magnetic, cheerful personality, he was always the most loved person in the room. The thing is, he told me that he had identified a purpose bigger than himself to stay alive – and that was me. He wanted to see me grow up. Some days were harder than others. I often saw him in extreme pain, and towards the end he had to use a wheelchair to get around. Every medical check-up would undoubtedly cause a level of anxiety. But my dad was willing to use what time he had left to embrace the beauty of life's possibilities. He chose to tap into a higher power, harnessing an energy that is within us all, just as I do. I'm not trying to say that embracing possibility healed my dad; but having goals and manifesting allowed him to live in the moment and truly enjoy the time he had left.

He died in my arms when I was nineteen years old, and I am forever thankful that he knowingly programmed me to believe in myself, to love a higher power and expect the world to love me back.

I believe that change actually starts from within, yet we are so primed to look outside of us for answers. Seeing my dad's determination in the face of great adversity, I came up with a theory. If my dad could continue to see possibility in the depths of a terminal illness, then so could I. I asked myself: if I focus on welcoming joyful abundance in all areas of my life, how far can I go?

It turns out, *very* far. And I owe it to all of you to put these techniques into practice. Tapping in means you're becoming a master of your own mind, the boss of your brain and the harnesser of your heart.

YOUR SUBCONSCIOUS MIND CAN'T TAKE A JOKE . . . AND KNOWING THIS WILL CHANGE YOUR LIFE.

The thrust of tapping (certainly the way I approach it within Rapid Tapping) is about remastering the 'coding' running in your subconscious mind. I use the terms pre-programmed, default and coding interchangeably, and most of this is due to the subconscious part of the mind. The truest definition might be exactly what it implies: it's *sub*conscious, meaning you aren't aware of what's happening beneath the surface of your multilayered mind, or what I call your 'consciousness' layers.

Basically, your subconscious mind doesn't get inference, subtle clues or emojis. It just does what it knows. It doesn't argue with you. It knows no right or wrong. It has no empathy or bad blood with you for something you did once when you were drunk. It autopilots your life by holding all the information it requires to keep you alive, and regurgitates it. Your subconscious mind is similar to your belief system in that way: they both just get on with things, calling all the shots. Can you imagine what's going on automatically in your own subconscious mind, without you even consciously knowing? Tons.

If you're anything like me, you simply cannot resign yourself to the way things currently are within your subconscious mind. Why? Because the contents of your subconscious mind might not match up to your wild, exciting vision for your future possibilities ... and no matter how much you *think* you want something and *do* things to try and make it all happen, you won't easily manifest it if you're not congruent in all your levels of consciousness.

Understanding your mind and acknowledging what it's capable of is to become proficient at modern manifestation.

THE LAYERS OF CONSCIOUSNESS

Psychologists, therapists, scientists and mystics have various definitions of how consciousness breaks down. I can only offer up my own here, which is informed by my dad, my own life and centuries upon centuries of science and spiritual pioneering. I believe that I am *always* learning; if we can maintain the attitude of a beginner we will stay open-hearted and pioneering. I suspect I'll upset many a Jungian advocate or slip up on Freud; forgive me. I've studied their work to degree level and it's fabulous, but I like to think that we can offer up our own authentic truth that adds to the conversation. We are each capable of being a unique messenger that interprets in a fresh way.

Here's how I look at the relationship between the layers of consciousness and desires, goals and visions. Let's say you have a goal right now, or something you want. Here's what's actually going down beneath the surface of that desire.

- **Consciously** I am aware that I WANT it.
- **Subconsciously** I CREATE it.
- **Unconsciously** I BLOCK it.
- **Superconsciously** I AM it.

Your conscious and subconscious are learned beliefs and behaviours. They're the pre-programmed parts you can tap into to create the most audacious of goals. Your unconscious and superconscious layers are innate because you were born with them. They're the mysteries we can tap into to feel truly fulfilled and at peace with our multifaceted essence, and how we belong in this incredible, kind universe. I'm going to break down each layer one by one.

Conscious mind – aka The Wanter

The tiny part of our being that is conscious, active and known. It's where we think things up, and we *want* from here. It's where the desires such as 'I want to get a promotion', 'I can start my own business doing what I love' or 'I can lose weight and kick the chocolate habit' are formed.

Here's the absolute killer when it comes to manifesting, and a massive reason why I advocate the power of tapping. As we know, very few of our thoughts are conscious, and yet we spend so much time *wanting* in our heads, wishing for stuff and making sense of it. Here's the thing: your conscious mind is useful, but certainly not the be all and end all of making stuff happen.

Most of our emphasis is on our conscious mind, but this is limited living. How can you use it to identify and clear a block or limiting belief when most of your day-to-day thoughts are stored elsewhere? Remember when I told you how your mind is able to handle eleven million bits of information per minute? Well, out of that, your conscious 'thinking' part is responsible for about forty to fifty useful bits, which is quite frankly rather lame.

So you can't use your conscious mind to talk yourself into something. Neither can you talk yourself out of believing something about yourself. You know full well that *wanting* to take a leap and actually *doing* it are two different things. To use an analogy here: it's like screaming at your TV to stop playing *Below Deck* on Netflix and expecting it to switch itself off. You are using the wrong system and wasting all your energy. You need to press a button on your remote control to stop the reality TV infecting your mind and numbing your life (only joking – I have produced entertainment shows – but you get what I'm saying!).

So the conscious mind is totally overpowered by the subconscious mind. It's a scary thought – but I just want to reiterate that there's so much going on under the surface. And despite all this being scientifically proven, we are stubbornly trying to operate within the tip of our own iceberg (instead of the juggernaut underneath). When I start working with clients, I find they blame themselves for lacking determination, resilience and willpower. We ask ourselves the same questions: Why didn't I do the work I knew I was meant to? Why am I still afraid to get into a long-term relationship? Why am I getting triggered by my successful friend and failing miserably? This sucks, but you don't have to live with all this self-doubt and guilt (it's that coding, again) if you start to make your conscious mind BFFs with your subconscious mind. They just need to be on the same page. The conscious mind can flourish if it is directed properly with unwavering focus. Tapping is what helps you do that, and once you get this you won't be able to stop! By consciously thinking sustained thoughts that propel you towards your life vision – and by using your conscious wording to affirm the possibility of this – you're getting closer to your goals.

So, ease up on yourself. You're a human filing cabinet and we need to declutter your old paperwork and get you onto a MacBook Pro.

Subconscious mind – aka The Creator

The 95 per cent mainframe of where we manifest from. The big one. The huge mothership behind every move we make. That Rolodex of information being stored to make our life safer and simpler so we can make decisions in nanoseconds and not have to wake up every day and learn everything again.

Of course, we need this. Who wants to wake up each day and have to consciously remember the stuff we've come to learn instinctively? Without it we would walk across a road without a care in the world, end up getting knocked over and that would be it for this lifetime. Our subconscious mind is teeing up basic survival signals all the time like 'Danger, don't cross when cars are around' or 'Run! You're being chased by a tiger.' Your body follows suit accordingly.

But as well as keeping us safe from fast cars and tigers, our subconscious also stores our earliest beliefs of what we consider to be right–wrong, safe–unsafe, good–bad. Growing up, we are actively building a belief blueprint that is informed by our environment and caregivers to help us make sense of the world. The problem is that we continue to draw on this unreliable guide throughout our lives. But just going along with this old information is yielding us minuscule results by comparison.

We will *always* need to bypass the conscious mind and move towards our subconscious in order to change our perceptions. Just ask any hypnotherapist that. The big part of the iceberg compared with the tip of it, remember? Or you can think of it as the dirty-looking engine under the bonnet of a snazzy shiny car being where all the power comes from. Learn how it works or get a decent mechanic and you can actually *drive* that snazzy car rather than it sitting pretty on the road going nowhere fast.

Unconscious mind – aka The Blocker

The deepest level of the subconscious, and the longest thread from the conscious. It can even carry imprints from previous generations that can block you if you don't engage with and nurture it. However, it is your all-knowing and wise friend that is working for your highest good. It is like a seed of your essence, carrying all the information necessary for you to bloom. The wise part of your mind–body, connected to you in your human form. It does the hard work of healing for us, if we allow it to – and we can trust that it only gives us as much as we can handle. So we don't have to 'think' our way to a restoration of energetic flow and we can return to love.

This is where tapping really holds up as an energy therapy, because by surrendering some control of your thinking mind, you're inviting your wise unconscious to lead you. This is freeing because even just tapping without words can help you feel more connected to your own essence, and encourage you to appreciate your time on this planet. Try it now.

Tapping exercise: Unconscious Connection

1 Close your eyes and bring your entire body to your mind's eye. From your feet to the top of your head and everything in between, each bone and cell within it.
2 Now imagine you are lifting up above that body. See if you can hover lightly above that body, those bones and those cells.
3 Now from this new, heightened perspective look at that body and see if you can let your unconscious pick a new shape or colour, or anything you can easily communicate with. What do you see forming?
4 Now tap gently all around that new formation, as if you're nurturing all the energy it's wisely holding for you. You're just quietly tapping without words. You're acknowledging anything that's hidden within, allowing it to be seen and heard, to be nurtured like a seed. What beautiful possibilities exist within this for you, waiting to come into fruition?
5 Tap quietly as you focus gratefully on this essence of you.

You can't hear it, smell it, touch it, taste it, granted. But you can sense it if you meditate into the moment and suspend your disbelief in the unknown. Take dogs, for example: dogs can hear frequencies that are undetectable to the human ear. They hear what we don't hear. Does what they're hearing exist? Yes, of course. And now we have the technology to prove it, but that wasn't always the case. I think of the unconscious in a similar way: it's the depth that we can't easily prove or access yet, which makes it a sweet little mystery all of our own.

It is the part of you that regulates your existence without you having to think about it; you don't know how your cells work, you don't need to. How do we know to automatically squirm towards a nipple when we are born? It's just something in us.

Superconscious mind – aka The Everything

Ah, the beautiful layer of our consciousness that is so *outside* of us yet simultaneously *inside* of us. It's the Whole. The 'I Am'. The Everything. Pure flow. It's away from time and space, in a level of quantum possibility. It's the purest form of energy where 'All is All', as *The Kybalion*, a book thought to be based on Ancient Egyptian teachings, would say.

To hack into this energetic realm within your consciousness is to truly supercharge your potential, but it's also important to acknowledge that this is not part of your body. This is what I call the 'Infinite Mind' or the 'Big Mind', unhindered by the interference of a human shell. It extends beyond your body and old understanding of Newtonian science; like Alice in her Wonderland, you're into the magical world of the unexplained. I believe this superconscious part of our mind is divinely connected to an energy that I like to call 'God Source Energy' but can be called whatever you like – The Universe, The Force, Big Magic. The point is that if you want to harness the full benefits of what tapping can do, you need to be open to the existence of something other than our flesh and blood. This is the higher power I've spoken about before – the place where your higher self has been there, done that and got the T-shirt.

We will go on to discover that our reality isn't actually fixed, it's fluid. If you've not delved into new science, prepare to be gobsmacked. Chances are you aren't a quantum physicist, so later in the book we'll cover basic quantum theory in greater detail as it's very relevant when it comes to manifesting our best lives. Are we solid, orderly and exactly as we believe things to be, or is there something more malleable going on? A quantum, or what I call a 'possibility' approach to life, tells us what we experience exists in a big haze of potential options and levels of probability, which you can tap into and access by using determined focus. If you've ever seen the film, *Sliding Doors*, you'll know that the main character Gwyneth Paltrow experiences two different versions of the same life. Well, superconsciousness tells us that life is like a massive epic, unending version of this all going on at once in some magical realm. Except it isn't magic, it's new science.

This is my truth around the definition of energetics, and I urge you to come to your own definition of superconsciousness. Can't get your head around it yet? That's OK. Our logical mind tries to methodically understand it, but it is not to be understood, only experienced. Try telling an eight-year-old that one day they'll probably enjoy going to the pub, downing five shots and being left with a hangover – only to do it all again the next day. They're at the mercy of their own understanding. Try telling an eighteen-year-old considering university life (like my son as I write this) the same thing and they're more able to sense the possibility of it.

The point is that if you surrender your (over-)thinking mind and faithfully start to use the contents of this book to manifest your life – and you brush up on the basics of quantum physics – then anything *is* possible. Successful manifestors defy rationale and logic. Because nothing is impossible: it's all there already, waiting to become our reality. In the superconscious realm we are free from the interference of the other parts of our consciousness like painful memories, so if we start to access possibility on a more regular basis through techniques such as tapping then we feel more able to attract abundance into our lives. The awakening of intuition, the connection to God Source Energy – and how much we surrender ourselves to the guidance of this is in direct proportion to the health of the soul. I have seen this over and over with clients. If we could be taught as children to connect to our soul and not place so much focus on the limited vessel we have in our human form, we might be a lot happier. With tapping, we can upgrade our whole consciousness 'coding' and really go for it in life!

HOW TO ACKNOWLEDGE AND UPGRADE YOUR CODING

It's important to take your coding seriously and to make sure you're resetting the balance as often as you can by tapping out the negative patterns you've learned over the years. It's about clearing out and tapping *in* the new coding you want to adopt so that your subconscious mind matches up with your conscious goals and vision for your future. Most of the time it's likely that the two won't match up, as your subconscious mind will go directly to your learned response and you end up thrown into what is known as conscious conflict. This is when the conscious part of you says,

'I desperately want to do that!', while the autopilot part of you argues, 'There's no way that's possible.' And, in the war between conscious and subconscious, the latter *always* wins

What coding would you need to have to make your dreams a reality?

CASE STUDY: FARAH NAZEER

For example take my client, Farah Nazeer, politician and chief executive officer of the charity Women's Aid, which champions the liberation of women and girls from domestic violence. In her role, she deals with the government and national media on a daily basis, so it's fair to say she's experienced her fair share of stress.

Farah first came to me after she was asked to make an innovative speech. Although she was passionate about the subject and initially thought, 'Hell, yes!', a coded gremlin immediately countered with, 'Oh god no, I can't do that. I'm actually not good enough for that. I can't do it.' Her subconscious mind took over and limited her potential to deliver an amazing, impactful speech (cue nerves and sweaty palms!). The truth is Farah was perfectly capable of going on stage, but the stress of the situation had overwhelmed her. Her brain listened to the signals of rising panic from her nervous system and all of her accomplishments, experience and ability went out the window. So I shared a tap with Farah designed to ease her stress that allowed her not only to give the speech, but even to wow the crowd.

After Farah's positive experience, her fundamental coding was updated as her brain registered the new evidence that it was well within her power to captivate an audience. Farah has since told me that she is now able to approach and communicate with the media with renewed ease – and she's also noticed tangible upswings in her work overall. Like most people who tap, Farah needs to keep up with it regularly to help deal with life's daily stressors. Remember, if you're disciplined with your tapping – even if it's only a few minutes at a time – it will come to your rescue in SOS moments when you want to rapidly shift into a positive energy.

So what will you do? Stay true to old patterns, or be brave and upgrade?

THE SEVEN CODES OF CHANGE

It's not just tapping that can help you transform. When I want to upgrade a part of my life, I have found that we can alter the 'codes' in seven key areas.

1 Self-talk – inner and outer

Self-talk is one of the most dangerous weapons we own. And we use it liberally and without mercy. If we are cruel rather than kind to ourselves, it negatively changes our energy and shapes our identity every time we do it. If this is you, it can be helpful to track your self-talk in a diary, noting your inner and outer self-talk in two long lists.

- List all the negative things you say about yourself to others (*outer self-talk*)
- List all the negative things you say to yourself in your head (*inner self-talk*)
- Now call a friend and direct all of that at her.

Mean isn't it? It would make them feel bad. Now imagine you keep saying these things over and over to your friend. It's likely that they'd start to believe you. Her subconscious would be matching all sorts of evidence to reinforce that it *must* be true and her entire energy and behaviours may change accordingly.

The Self-Talk Challenge

This may be an uncomfortable and difficult exercise, but it can help to really identify how you talk about yourself.

1   Take the list you created of both your inner and outer self-talk and record yourself reading all the things you have written down.
2   Listen back to your recording.

This is what you are nourishing yourself with. You are not giving yourself a chance to break free unless you stop it. Your subconscious is overloaded with this false information. (PS You're good enough. You're exceptional. You're part of the universe's life blood. You can have the life you want, actually.)

2 Environment

Be ruthless about taking time out to be in a better place and space, more conducive to what you want to feel. The moments in your life add up because you're teaching your body how to act depending on the information that's coming in from your environment – and this doesn't really always work in our favour! Especially if we are not creating new learnings and experiences. If we just do and think the same things every day, we can't stimulate our subconscious and we end up stuck. No surprise then that it's hard to *create* new stuff if we don't *do* new stuff.

Write down three ways you can upgrade your environment. Do something different, go somewhere new – maybe it's even as simple as changing your route to work. How about using feng shui to maximise the energy in your home, or smudging white sage to neutralise the negative energy of previous owners? Could you switch your phone off before bed and opt for an alarm clock that uses light to calmly wake you instead? Even small steps transform your coding.

3 Beliefs

Beliefs will bring *you* down if you don't bring *them* down. Systematically tap each day. Disprove and debunk as many false beliefs as you can by asking the question, 'Is this ultimately true, for everyone, in all contexts, always?' If the answer is no, it's not a fact. It's a belief and you can change your perception of it. You can also start to ditch the people and places that stop you from believing in your own potential. Why tolerate naysayers? It's your life, not theirs. Believe in yourself.

4 Imagination

Take actual time to imagine. Daydream. Think about what *could* be rather than what *has* been. Be a bit more Disney dreamer and connect to the part of you that used to spend time thinking of the fun stuff. Maybe you could go on a creative writing course, or try painting? Spending time 'hands on' will open you up to new ways of being – remember, it's not all about work. Write down three things that help you feel inspired. Then make a pact with yourself to carve out time to actually do them.

5 Visualisation

Take time out to visualise and mentally rehearse your meetings, difficult conversations and future self. What does it feel like? What does it look like? Become a master at creative visualisation by noticing as much detail as you can and practising mindful moments. You have a very visual brain, so use it wisely by embedding visions of what you might manifest; go wild and daydream like a child might. Somewhere along the lines, we've all stopped listening to our inner child. Journal on this: what would my inner child love to make believe could happen in my life, if it was easy to make that a reality? Then see if you can paint a picture of this, like a story in your head. When you do this, you increase energetic resonance to that idea. If you don't allow yourself to dream into the future, you stay in the past.

6 Affirmations

Spend time on these each day. I will later teach you how to create effective affirmations and incorporate them into your lifestyle.

Most of the time, unplanned affirmations don't work the way you want them to, so plan them correctly and tap them in.

7 Brain power

Change your brain by understanding how it works and what you can do to alter patterns; how can you use tapping to start sending signals that support your calmest, most confident self.

We now know that it's possible for existing synapses to adapt, and that our brain is constantly creating new connections based on our experienced environment. This is a huge discovery, as for centuries we were taught that our brain is a fixed entity. It isn't.

YOUR SECRET BRAIN POWER – AND HOW TO USE IT

Now we're getting into the brainy part of the book. I'm no neuroscientist but I love the brain; and it's intrinsic to modern manifesting. If you really want to tap into what you're capable of achieving in this life, in your body, then it goes much further than a dreamcatcher. You're actually a little neuro-machine, with a powerful brain.

Let's go back to 1964. If I were alive then I'd have had a female crush on Professor Marian Diamond, a ballsy, incredibly renowned neuroscientist, who had just published a landmark paper that demonstrated for the first time the idea of neuroplasticity. Her findings proved that your brain didn't just decay and shrink as you aged, it could actually form new synaptic connections depending on your experiences in your given environment. This shocked the world in the same way quantum physics shocked Einstein.

Thanks to Marian Diamond (who was initially a target of ridicule and faced gender discrimination as a young female pioneer in a sea of male contemporaries) we can apply this accepted concept to modern manifesting in a proven, clinical way. As Robert Knight, a professor at UC Berkeley, where Diamond taught for over fifty years, told *The Washington Post*, 'The idea that the brain could change based on environmental input and stimulation was felt to be silly . . . And that's the boat she completely sank.' Woop.

WHY IS NEUROPLASTICITY IMPORTANT TO TAPPING INTO YOUR BEST LIFE?

The *Oxford English Dictionary* defines neuroplasticity as:

> *'The ability of the nervous system to form and reorganise connections and pathways, as during development and learning or following injury.'*

Sounds boring, but in the Poppy Delbridge dictionary it's pretty much defined as 'the gateway to manifestation'. Neuroplasticity, as outlined from Diamond's discoveries, revealed what our emotions, memories and learning capacity looked like in terms of the way our brain worked. We suddenly had proof that our brains don't stop developing when we're eighteen. We are not born with a set of fixed coded ways of being from our parents' genes that limit our possibilities or potential; we can modify connections in our brain and rewire them at any time, and see the results surprisingly quickly. We see this most obviously in injuries and recoveries, when rehabilitation catalyses the brain to relearn previous abilities by repairing old pathways or creating new ones. The interesting thing is that you can reorganise the brain in this way just as we now know we can reorganise beliefs and emotions, rapidly and quite simply. Tapping is a key way to encourage neuroplasticity but there are also other methods, such as the five key ways that Marian Diamond outlined.

Find an actionable up-level for each of these five areas and complete one per day on a working week. I've started you off with suggestions for each one.

Diet

When it comes to diet, we can increase our brain health by decreasing inflammation and eating foods that are proven to increase neuroplasticity, such as:

- Avocado
- Blueberries
- Broccoli
- Eggs
- Green leafy vegetables
- Olive oil
- Turmeric
- Walnuts

Exercise

This isn't just about achieving a toned body or escaping saggy knees, OK? Exercise increases blood flow and cell growth in the brain and also boosts memory. It wards off depression, helps you to see more possibilities in life and keeps you socially mobile too, as you'll be out and about.

Extra bonus if you're thinking about keeping your mind tip-top? Exercise improves fine motor coordination and brain connectivity, which can protect against cognitive decline.

Challenge

Don't waste your time on brain-numbing activities: challenge yourself. Maybe start that book you keep planning to read, apply to support your local council, be brave and plan a TEDx talk, or enrol in an online course you've been thinking about. To learn is to challenge.

Newness

Do something new every single day. Using new ways to promote neuroplasticity can rewrite the brain's story thus far and positively raise your frequency. Taking a life-drawing class, for example, activates the brain's default mode network, and this helps you create some 'brain rest', which is proven to improve creativity and to help you find new solutions to your emotional problems.

Love

A lovely one to add, I think, in a scientific paper. This is so relevant to our work here because to love is to activate not only your heart but also your entire relevance in the big old universe, which is beating as one massive heart, interwoven and interconnected. Tap into that and see what happens. Bestselling author and researcher in neuroscience, Dr Joe Dispenza, talks about the heart quite a lot in relation to the brain. He says that when our heart is not in a dialogue with our brain we are not operating on full congruent flow. Have you ever noticed that your heart feels one thing but your mind or 'head' feels another? That's incongruence and it stresses out our body.

'Our brain receives many of its instructions on what to do from the heart. Studies show that the heart is able to think, feel, and have emotions on its own.'

Research has shown that our heart might even be more powerful than our brain when it comes to signalling our reactions. This is mammoth. Please follow your heart's desires.

TAPPING AND YOUR BRAIN

Rather than thinking of our brain as one mass, an overwhelming entity, understand that the brain has different sections, each with individual roles to play in the whole. It's working closely with the nervous system, the command centre. The most useful region to know about when it comes to tapping is the brain's limbic system, which is the emotion- and memory-processing zone. It's where we process the way we feel, the arousal we might feel, the learning we lean into and the memories we store. The two main structures relevant to tapping are called the **amygdala** (aka The Stresser) and the **hippocampus** (aka The Rememberer).

What is the amygdala?

The little almond-shaped region of the brain that is responsible for sending us into fight-or-flight mode, and the freeze and faint modes too. We know this is a major signaller to the rest of our body and it's responsible for anxiety, heightened cortisol production, rushes of adrenalin and stress!

Something happens, someone irritates you and then 'Bam!' – you go into overdrive. It's actually arousal, but not the sexy kind. An aroused amygdala hijacks everything and has one rule: kill or be killed. Your immunity shuts down (because when you're running or fighting, you're not interested in fighting off the flu) and you use every ounce of adrenalin to stay alive. You're surviving. Your human energy is totally wiped out.

The sad thing is we're living in this mode by default now, in a state of fear brought about by past experiences or cultural stress. It takes its toll on our mind, spirit and physical health.

As health writer and researcher Dawson Church writes in his fabulous book, *Bliss Brain*:

'The [amygdala is the] brain's fire alarm . . . in stressed people. The circuit sends signals from the amygdala to the prefrontal cortex, hijacking the brain's decision-making centres and paralysing executive function.'

We just can't make rational or clear decisions when the amygdala is overreacting on our behalf, usually uselessly. When we lived as cave dwellers, thousands of years ago, we were constantly in real danger so we just had one thing to focus on: survival. Now we mistake a tricky journey or one bad review as real danger. It's still psychological stress, but it isn't actually survival – we just still think it is. It doesn't serve us to keep this part of our brain in hyper mode.

'Most of us are living today as if it were yesterday.'
DR JOE DISPENZA, *What the Bleep*

When the body is not getting its needs met, it tells the brain and the brain's role is to warn our nervous system, which then thinks: should we let it slide or do we need to protect? Let's deviate for a moment to unravel this.

What is the nervous system?

The nervous system controls everything we do. It's made up of your brain, spinal cord and nerves. These nerves send messages to and

from the body to the brain so that we can make sense of what is
going on and respond with appropriate action.

'Oh, you're getting on my nerves!' my grandma used to say all
the time. As a successful female manager working in the busy,
male-dominated Royal dockyards in the 1970s, perhaps she
needed a little de-stress after a long day's work. She needed to
know about meditation, yoga, tapping and all the amazing practices and apps we now have to help us calm down. As a society
we're giving more time to self-care and meditation than we used
to, and there's less stigma around looking after our mental health,
certainly, but our bodies haven't quite caught up yet. We still have
an automated nervous-system reaction that often makes us feel
intense stress when it's not necessary. Perhaps this is a hang-up
from when we were faced with life-or-death situations every day.
As my mum used to remind me, 'Poppy, it's not life or death, get
over it.' But that's the last thing you want to hear when you feel
like it is. Tapping helps you gain control of this feeling and how
you respond to it.

Our nervous system can be broadly separated into two camps:
the **sympathetic** and the **parasympathetic**.

The sympathetic system is the one we're switching off when we
tap: it's the fight-or-flight response that keeps you alive and shows
you 'sympathy' by instantly flooding your system with adrenalin
and cortisol and dopamine (the catecholamines) which are there
for temporary survival purposes. It's not so sympathetic actually.
Stressful living is linked to unwanted visible side effects such as
acne, sweating and hair loss, but making time for tapping will
effectively help combat these problems.

The parasympathetic mode, however, is more chilled because it's
all about actions that don't need you to respond quickly. It's often
called the 'rest-and-digest' division.

We are so used to being in hyper mode with low-level stress chemicals pumping through our body that our brain thinks it's doing us a favour by responding to the nerve signals that say 'Oi, alert panic mode' when we trigger an old wound like seeing an ex, running out of time in the day, making a minor mistake at work. So the brain flashes pictures to the frontal lobe and tries to find reminders and matches for what has come before. So are we addicted to being stuck in the sympathetic nervous system within our negative emotional states? Dr Joe Dispenza thinks so. He tells us that we are so addicted to stress that we stay exactly where we've always been – in the past, in the throes of stress. He believes that we can't make choices properly because just like a dog (which has a small frontal lobe), we bark – and remain in a constant low-vibrational state instead of throwing ourselves into new experiences that could allay our anxieties.

We know through research that interrupting the nervous system helps to reduce this stress almost instantly and significantly, hence 'rapid tapping'. Stress not only stops logic, it can also shrink the bit of our brain responsible for rational reasoning. That's why when you've had a holiday you can 'think straight', or you have ideas creatively pop into your head when you're swimming, or taking a lovely walk in nature.

Stress hormones can be very unknowingly and sneakily addictive. We can create all sorts of body reactions and illness when we are stressed, so by not paying attention to our repeated thoughts, the ones we dwell on, we will be stuck in the same place, in the same pattern, and our adrenal response will kick in and keep on depleting us. I often wonder if this is what brought down my dad when he became ill. Perhaps he just really wanted to succeed for his family and didn't even *know* how stressed he was.

One of my clients, a high-flying financial advisor, confessed that she was suffering from depression but didn't want to acknowledge her mental state as it made her feel like a failure. This is totally unhelpful because a) she's human, not a machine and b) to avoid our basic emotional responses over time causes chronic energetic stress, which can lead to or exacerbate symptoms of depression. Those of us who have experienced depression are at risk of future bouts of it, and this is more likely when we're faced with stress.

Scientists have found that depressed patients show ongoing inflammation in the hippocampus and that chronic stress can reduce the production of our well-being hormone, serotonin, which modulates our mood. Depression is no joke: it's debilitating and things like making decisions, problem-solving and planning become difficult. It also creates an attention bias to negativity, a habitual issue that will gain momentum and negatively change your brain, according to neuroplasticity. On top of that, if we don't interrupt the pathways of the amygdala, we release *more* cortisol, which means we won't be able to sleep properly and our circadian rhythms go AWOL. Long-term elevation in cortisol levels can lead to:

- Adrenal fatigue
- Low energy/mood
- Insomnia
- Weaker immune systems
- Forgetfulness/an inability to focus
- Exhaustion and burnout
- Premature ageing

We can use tapping to help alleviate these symptoms, as shown in a 2019 study published in the *Journal of Evidence-Based*

Integrative Medicine that explored how EFT can improve our over-all well-being. Researchers found that the practice can:

- Reduce signs of anxiety by almost 60 per cent.
- Reduce blood cortisol (stress hormone) levels by 43 per cent on average.
- Cause a 68 per cent drop in the experience of physical pain.
- Alleviate the symptoms of PTSD in eight out of ten veterans after only six hours of therapy (these results were sustained over follow-up appointments).
- Improve people's general happiness by 31 per cent.
- As a happy side-effect, it has also been shown to reduce cravings by up to 74 per cent.

Memory like a hippocampus

But tapping goes deeper than treating symptoms. It tackles the underlying issue too. Who has memories? All of us! Some we want, some we don't. The hippocampus is the part of the brain in charge of them, plus our new learning. We need memories so we don't get knackered trying to remember everything all the time – they're nature's short cuts – but they're depriving us of a lot of beautiful scenery too. When we take something in as information, the hippocampus analyses it and decides whether it's worth being stored in our long-term memory.

How many of your memories are happy? Many studies suggest that our brain is biased towards unhappy memories as well as neg-ative thought-loops. The more depressing the experience, the more stable the memory becomes, and this gives it a huge leg-up regarding how we make decisions. This is an evolutionary response but also energetic – you remember *not* to do something again if it was a rub-bish experience or made you feel bad. It's a pre-approved pattern that leads to healthy or unhealthy addictions, behaviours and phobias.

Sadly we can't change our actual memories by tapping (I still remember the time I pulled out a tampon instead of a sweet on my first date), but we can definitely reduce the emotional charge behind them and deactivate the negativity of the attached response (I no longer feel the mortifying embarrassment attached to said tampon experience). The worrying thing is that over time, if we are chronically stressed or depressed, our hippocampus actually *shrinks*. It can also start to calcify, because cortisol released from the amygdala is deposited here. No thanks.

Cultivating 'newness', as prescribed by Marian Diamond, is imperative because if we don't stimulate a bit of grey matter, we regurgitate all the old bullshit over and over again, like 'I can't possibly do that' or 'I'm not as good as Sarah because this that and the other memory.' You might catch an old Disney movie you watched in a hypnotic state as a five-year-old and remember that you weren't pretty enough to have a prince of your own. You might remember that time your caregiver told you as a child that you were stupid. Or to be quiet. Or that your sister was smarter than you. These memories trigger emotions.

'Emotions determine the quality of our lives. They occur in every relationship we care about – in the workplace, in our friendships, in dealings with family members, and in our most intimate relationships. They can save our lives, but they can also cause real damage.'

PAUL EKMAN, world-renowned psychologist
and author of *Emotions Revealed*

Studies have shown that just hearing a triggering word can cause a rapid reaction, which can totally derail us emotionally. This means you might hear someone call you 'lazy' and you retaliate or feel awful because you've heard it before and your brain scans for the memory of the emotional energy stored behind the word. I am interested to see further research on how this works both ways. If your brain can make you feel bad simply by hearing words, perhaps it can make you feel good too?

One study into the embodiment of emotions found that first-person positive feelings such as 'my happiness' gave a more intense effect than more general positive words like 'her happiness'. Unsurprisingly, negative words came out much higher on the intensity scale when they were related to the self – 'my horrible day' as opposed to 'his horrible day', for example – suggesting that speaking to ourselves purposefully and consciously deepens the effect (good and bad) of subjective emotions. In other words, although tapping is a somatic therapy where the body plays a big role, and energy is central to the concept, *what* we say and *how* we say it is why I often encourage you to 'fill in the blanks' within the Rapid Tapping scripts. This is also why affirmations have their very own chapter later on. Words are power.

So how can we be the boss of our brain's hippocampus to prepare for effective manifesting? 'Use it or lose it!', as Professor Diamond says about the brain's ability to change your life. The same concept applies as soon as we tap into a state of possibility: we need to make use of a positive state of mind as soon as we've accessed it, then create a new memory within the hippocampus by keeping our brain malleable and active. This means doing new things, facing our fears and taking creative leaps. A 2012 study found evidence to support the idea that picking up a new language increases grey matter density and neuroplasticity. After three months of intensive study of a new topic, fourteen adult interpreters saw increases in both grey matter density and hippocampal volume. So it's important that we keep trying to learn and create new experiences – even just making a tiny change to our daily routine – regardless of whether or not we fail. When I think of my dad, I can't help but recall the sheer number of new experiences he brought into his life; he rarely repeated a day in the same way. From driving me to school on a new route, to becoming a black belt in martial arts, he understood the power of neuroplasticity.

The more we can repeat the new, the more it is reinforced within our brain and we can combat our bias towards negative memories.

> **HACK:** A useful way to combat negative bias is to create a list of five happy memories. Throughout the day, visualise each of your chosen memories in your mind, replaying every detail as if it's happening right that moment. Remember, your brain doesn't know the difference between reality and imagination, so it will believe it's happening again.

That's why you'll often hear me say 'repeat to reinforce' in Rapid Tapping, because our intention must be to override the old negative dross and create new neural pathways that lead to fresh possibilities, rather than pre-perceived pessimism about our potential. Perception is absolutely not the same as fact; if we've perceived something it doesn't make it universally true for all. I'll share with you the best journal prompt ever: *is it universally and ultimately true for all people, in all contexts?* If the answer is no, it is perception. Hallelujah.

But here's the kicker about our brain's ability to hold negative information. Neuroscience tells us that we are like a sponge, soaking up information until we get to the age of seven. Our brain waves are in a different, more impressionable mode and we are neurologically more open. We take in information so super easily that we're literally being programmed for the rest of our life – but unless we address it, we become static and stagnant holding the same information. This becomes entangled information of course, affecting the heart on an emotional level. If you want to delve further into this idea, read *The Book You Wish Your Parents Had Read (And Your Children Will Be Glad You Did)*, by my friend psychotherapist Philippa Perry – you can also learn a ton about how to consciously parent. She says of emotions:

'This is what a child needs: for a parent to be a container for their emotions. This means you are alongside them and know and accept what they feel but you are not being overwhelmed by their feelings.'

Being able to be a 'container' means witnessing anger in a child, understanding why they are angry and perhaps putting that into words for them, finding acceptable ways for them to express their anger and not being punitive or overwhelmed by the anger. The same is true for your friends, your loved ones and your own emotions too.

I am not sure any of us have been spared a harsh word, some false information or a person of authority lodging horrible memories into us. But try answering this question: would you honestly consciously choose to create your life again and say yes to anxiety, stress, anger issues, body pain, trauma?

No, you would not. You haven't chosen it consciously. We all just experience it. So where is it all coming from? Well, my feeling is that there is a lot of subconscious stuff taking the driving seat and there's more we could do to consciously guide our subconscious into some new patterns to help free us, not only emotionally but in the whole realm of life. Our brains don't know how easy it is to upgrade. Likewise, there's so much happening in the shadows of the unconscious waiting to be healed. Add to that a commonplace misunderstanding of tapping into our innate energetic power ... it's no wonder we feel 'on default'.

Stuff has happened in your past – and maybe even in your day today – but there's still a new way ahead. Try this quick and simple Big 'But' Tap routine, which will make you feel more ready to take those action steps you've been putting off.

Tapping exercise: The Big 'But' Tap

1 Take a big, deep breath in through your nose and exhale through your mouth.
2 Repeat this with me as you tap through the Rapid Tapping points:

- I acknowledge that life has thrown me some curveballs BUT I am able to influence my life positively now.
- I acknowledge my emotional attachments and stresses BUT I am choosing to enter a new realm of possibility.
- I acknowledge I've not understood the full power of my subconscious BUT I am working with it now.
- There's a part of me that has been pre-programmed negatively BUT I am becoming fully aware of how powerful I actually am.

- Maybe it hasn't been easy for me previously BUT I made it, and I am seeing new evidence each day that brings me into harmony, opportunity and love.
- Maybe an upgrade has felt impossible before BUT I am choosing to be fully infinite in my power now.
- Maybe things were different before BUT I am able to choose again right now.
- I might still feel overwhelmed BUT it is possible for me to feel good.
- I might still feel burned out sometimes BUT it is possible for me to use the power of my mind.
- I might still feel some fear BUT it is possible for me to see love and feel good.
- I may not have before BUT I acknowledge and honour myself right now.
- I am willing to take leaps in my life towards my goals, desires and visions!

GATHERING EVIDENCE (AND NOT FREAKING OUT ABOUT IT)

Now that you have a better understanding of our powerful minds and the part our brain plays in all this transformation work, you're ready to shift your life into heart-led, aligned and exciting success, on your terms!

Even though we are about to define the vision for your life and the way to structure your tapping to create goals, I'd invite you at this point to identify, accept and acknowledge that you're OK exactly as you are – you don't need to fix yourself. Instead, you can use the tools in this book to create new evidence for what might be possible for you. As we've learned, your brain is firing and wiring neurons all the time and in order to break the repeat cycle we can apply tapping.

Thinking of interrupting the cycle isn't the same; we're talking about a new brain-logged experience. Why do we sometimes freak out doing new things? Why do the fear goblins come to find us when we are out of our comfort zone?

It's not that we are not up to scratch – often it's not even imposter syndrome (which we *should* all feel, or we're not really growing as much as we could be) – instead it's chemical autopilot; our nervous system talking to our brain, which is trying hard to prove that new isn't good at all. It's all quite unsafe, neurologically speaking.

New equals potentially unsafe. Old equals proven to be familiar and therefore the best option. But it rarely is, unless we have gathered evidence throughout our childhood and early adolescence that would hold steadfast in a court of law that we are brilliant, able, capable and confident in all areas of our life. If that school existed, can you imagine the fees? It would be swamped. Instead we potter about doing the best we can, with the stored reactive patterns we created at the time.

Judge Judy, listen up – we're setting the record straight here. Your vision has nothing to do with past evidence. You can desire your heartfelt vision for the sake of the fundamental joy it brings you. It is your birthright to do so.

4 WHAT'S YOUR VISION?

I'm about to teach you how to clear the cobwebs of your memories and unhelpful evidence. But *why* are we clearing? As a coping strategy – or more than that? We are clearing in order to create our wildest goals, our deepest desires and our boldest vision! We are shifting paradigms. Remember: if it's not impossible, it's *possible*! So let's consider for a moment what you *do* want.

A vision for your life is like a super-umbrella term for all your desires and goals. Everything feeds into a vision, which guides your mindset around what's possible for you. Think you've got one? Think again. This probably goes far beyond anything you've done before. It's intricate. It's an art and a science. Get this right and you're in the slipstream to success. Get this wrong and you're pedalling uphill on a rusty, gearless bike wondering why it's so fucking difficult.

I teach vision and vision-board strategies to both individuals and companies – it's one of my favourite things to do – so to give you a taste of what you can achieve, I'll share some examples of my own envisioned manifestations:

- Vision: To live in LA for a while.
- Result: Being asked to executive produce a dating show I originated that had to be shot in California.

- Vision: To film the show in Malibu.
- Result: Shooting the show at the exact Malibu beach house that was on my vision board.

- Vision: To have a CEO corner office at work.
- Result: Inheriting a corner office that belonged to the CEO when the office space was rearranged.

- Vision: To live by the water with a view of two palm trees as depicted in one of my artworks.
- Result: Moving into my dream house that directly overlooks the Thames . . . with two palm trees clearly in view!

- Vision: To meet my soulmate.
- Result: Bumping into him after a series of detours on one particular day and discovering that he has the qualities I was looking for. Including that he wears linen shirts, with the sleeves rolled up (more on that later).

- Vision: To work with brands that I've dreamed of working with.
- Result: Working with Soho House, Bamford, Happy Place, the British Fashion Council and more.

- Vision: To become a published author.
- Result: Being approached by a literary agent, receiving multiple offers to write a book, and then signing the publishing deal for this very book.

Wherever you are right now, and whatever your level of self-belief, know that the continuous clearing work is bringing you closer to your vision. If you don't have a vision yet, don't worry; I'm about to explain some basic steps in my own vision system so you can create a powerful one of your own.

To get into the vibe, let's spend a moment in the future, just to play and get into the spirit of possibility. Imagine you've jumped ahead in your timeline of reality and you're looking back at a life you absolutely loved. What has happened? What was brilliant about what you did, who you were and the way you felt throughout your days?

Meditate, listen to music or take time in nature. Write down a few sentences, imagining that you're looking back on a life well lived, filled with true happiness and joy. Go wild! This can be a fun, creative exercise, but it can also be confronting to dig deep and think about all the things you actually want for yourself. Take some time to engage with your senses and mull over what you write down.

CREATING A POWERFUL VISION WITH MY VISION SYSTEM

I've built a whole system around creating a strong vision – and in Part Two, once you've worked on debunking and ditching old beliefs, you'll be ready to go deeper. To take things to the next level you may even want to take one of my courses, which you can find on my website (www.poppydelbridge.com). For now I would love you to keep your eye on the results you want to create for yourself, because lack of clarity can equate to a lack of direction.

I was at my friend Sarah's house one evening and I suggested that we spend the time sipping wine and creating a vision. She responded with, 'Oh I've got a vision, I'm fine. Look, I've had it laminated.' She showed me a bulleted list of about thirty targets that resembled a bucket list. Knowing exactly where you're headed by way of an imagined and envisioned future is not the same as a plan or set of rigid goals. Instead, imagine that you're creating a book to tell the story of your own life, chapter by chapter – you don't know all the details of each chapter yet, but you have an overarching narrative. In order to gain clarity around the story of your life, you'll need to let go of some parts that don't belong in your book. They're the things you've fallen into or tolerated, or parts of your life which no longer match the person you want to become. You'll also need to stop controlling and manipulating, because you really don't *know* how far your highest potential on this planet goes yet.

Creating a vision can be quite overwhelming, as we habitually downplay our desires and needs to the point where it's difficult to pinpoint what we want. So ask yourself: what is it that I truly want? Scary question. A lot of inner gremlins pop up because you're being invited to use the power of your truth, to call on your inner visionary, to engage with your daring dreamer, and unless these parts of you have been allowed to flourish in your childhood, relationships or career, it might feel like you're trying to wake the dead. But fear not, because you're already working towards becoming the most authentic version of yourself.

There are many elements within my vision system but I'd like to get you started with two key steps that will help you tap into the life you want: how to discover your values and how to use the 'Wheel of Possibility' to focus on your dream outcomes. These will help you create your own 'tapped in' vision manifesto.

LET'S BEGIN WITH VALUES

It is hugely relevant to be aware of our defining values when we set any goals for our life and career, and certainly when we are aligning more and more to our vision.

So what do I mean by values? They are a set of defining principles, which you consider to be true for you and important to the way you operate on a day-to-day basis at work and in life. If you practise the art of self-affirmation (which is really understanding what makes you tick, happy and connected – we'll touch on this in a later chapter), you're able to accept that a growth mindset is better for you than a negative, fixed one.

For example, I had a client who was a very dissatisfied CEO of a major corporation. She wanted my guidance with her vision: to become a board member of a Fortune 100 company. With this goal in mind I coached her, but when I asked her, 'If you were offered a role tomorrow, would you say "Hell, yes!" and take it immediately?' she broke down. We tapped as we talked. Her answer was no. She pretended to herself almost daily that she placed high value on being senior in her industry, but she actually realised her position of authority wasn't what she wanted at all. What she really craved was time with her children and an outlet for her creativity. She traced the desire to be accomplished back to a feeling that she had to prove herself to her overbearingly successful father. She ended up working her way up a ladder she didn't even really want to reach the top of; the truest values to her were actually 'creativity' and 'family'. She wasn't in alignment with her own needs or truest values so her vision wasn't authentic. It was compromised.

> **HACK:** If the answer to your question isn't a hell yes, it's a hell no.

This is why it's so important for us to be honest and discover more about ourselves with self-development and coaching – as well as tapping. When we live in accordance with our unique blend of what we value, we can start to flourish. Without knowing what these values are we can sometimes feel lost, frustrated and overwhelmed. Without living in congruence with our values we cannot realise our full potential and we don't feel that we are in manifesting flow.

So what are your truest, most authentic values in life? You can come up with your own, or go through this list and pick out the values that resonate most with you – when you tune in to them, they light up your heart:

- Accomplish
- Adventure
- Assemble
- Attract
- Beauty
- Bliss
- Breadwinner
- Build
- Change
- Communication
- Community
- Compassion
- Connection
- Contribute
- Create
- Danger
- Dare
- Direct
- Discern
- Discover
- Dominate
- Educate
- Emote
- Empathise
- Encourage
- Enlist

- Excellence
- Expertise
- Facilitate
- Family
- Feel
- Gamble
- Guide
- Hedonism
- Holidays
- Imagination
- Impact
- Improve
- Influence
- Inspire
- Instruct
- Intimacy
- Invent
- Kids
- Learn
- Maternal
- Nurture

- Observe
- Peace
- Perceive
- Persuade
- Physical
- Plan
- Power
- Provide
- Reign
- Risk
- Rule
- Sense
- Sensuality
- Serve
- Sex
- Sports
- Support
- The unknown
- Thrill
- Touch
- Win

Some of these values are intentionally similar to allow you to zone in on any patterns that might emerge, so let's narrow it down a bit to clarify and discover which values speak to you. As we've just learnt from my client's story, values should fill you with momentum and energy. If you're feeling like you *should* have something as a value but the thought of it is uninspiring, it's not a true honest value, so scrap it. Consistently trying to live your life to someone else's values will be detrimental to your manifesting and make you feel crap. Where's the point in that?

- What values do you consider to be important to the way you live, and which surprise you when others don't feel the same way?
- Which values make you feel powerful when you see them written down?
- What makes you feel truly satisfied in your working life?
- What makes you feel energised in your personal and family life?
- What brings you a genuine sense of purpose?

Now see if you can narrow it down to about five values.

HACK: At the end of each day, check in with yourself that you are making decisions based on these values. Try to identify examples of your five core values being honoured and if you can't, it's time to make adjustments in the way you spend your time.

Being at one with your core values is self-affirming so it increases self-worth, purpose and passion, allowing you to raise your frequency so you can manifest more effectively.

USING THE WHEEL OF POSSIBILITY

The second step I want to share with you is my philosophy about life: the Wheel of Possibility modality. It's similar to a life wheel, which is often used in coaching, but I've adapted it to fit the most common manifestation needs of my clients. When you're setting a massive, exciting vision for your life, it needs to feel truly 360°, incorporating everything from the way you feel emotionally to your physical well-being to your relationships and your work life. Each part of your life cannot operate independently, which is why I believe that trying to achieve work–life balance is a sham. It's about knowing it is fully possible to achieve unadulterated wholeness and integration.

That feels a bit overwhelming, though, doesn't it?

I'll explain how to use the Wheel of Possibility, so you can develop a fluid focus game plan. This often surprises my clients because at first they don't see the unexpected correlation between career progression and their physical body, or the impact of their love life on their finances. Your tapping routines work in the same way; you'll unknowingly improve an area of your life just by tapping into another. When it comes to mastering manifesting energetics, a win in one area is a win in all areas because your *baseline* rises. Likewise, it's impossible for one body part to operate alone as a single entity. Even the Bible spoke of this, so it's got a good 'oomph' behind it.

'Now the body is not made up of one part but of many. If the foot should say, "Because I am not a hand, I do not belong to the body" it would not for that reason cease to be part of the body.'
1 Corinthians 12

Stop trying to be separate and control each part of the whole at once. Your body isn't just an ear, in the same way that your whole life isn't your work. You can't forget your desire for a soulmate relationship until you're in a good place in your career. Life is now!

Something that may have a bearing on this tendency, when it comes to women, is the fact that generations of women have had to fight for their place in society – even to be recognised, in general.

Throughout history (even the name is penned by a man: *his*-story) women have not been given the same liberties as men; neither have women had it as easy as men when it comes to high-ranking roles in just about every industry you could imagine.

It's not surprising women have this ingrained belief that says they have to compromise – either be a mother *or* a CEO, either be a wife *or* a businesswoman. I'm saying that you *can* have both and you *can* have it all, but it's about focusing your energy on one life zone at a time and adjusting your mindset (built over generations) as we rise up into aligned wholeness.

I'm in a lucky position where I work with many incredible, change-making women, but even *they* have had to fight to be heard. Often to truly even hear themselves. Part of my job is to help my clients find their power and their voice – to help cut energetic cords of inequality we have had to deal with over decades. And that's just women; there are imbalances across social classes, ethnicity and sexuality too.

This idea of not being enough runs deep and it warps our belief systems and directs us away from what we should be spending our time on. For example, is it 'right' to focus on our career, but 'wrong' to focus on a relationship? It's 'necessary' to completely burn out in pursuit of recognition; it's 'unimportant' that we still haven't found the time to go on that three-day mini retreat we've been thinking about for the past five years.

HACK: Keep an eye on the big picture because it's the body holding the parts together, the 'big mind' in the superconscious that your 'little mind' is just a part of. That one imp on your shoulder telling you you're not good enough can be healed in pursuit of the bigger

vision. So where to start directing your attention?
My feeling is that you'll *know* when the time comes
intuitively – if you let it. You'll see synchronicities,
nudges, things will start to shift either by catastrophe
(when things fall apart) or by determined choice (which
you're making now by reading this book). So, let's begin.

Which area of your life will you choose to make whole and less
wonky first?

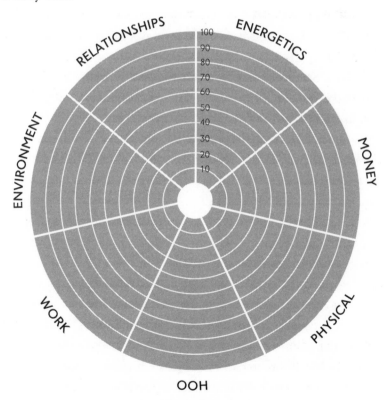

The Wheel of Possibility

The seven zones – or life areas – of the wheel are a useful framework to explore your envisioned life, but remember that each zone is still part of the greater circle of life. The idea is that having our desires met in each zone leads to an empowered, expansive life filled with possibilities. Using the wheel and tapping into zones as you go neutralises the overwhelm associated with trying to come up with one massive vision. So are you ready to level-up?

E = Energetics Your emotions, your energy, your mindset, and the way you manifest.

M = Money Your relationship to and your mindset around money and finances.

P = Physical Your body and what you put into it; your health and vitality.

O(oh) = Sex and your love relationship (because I needed to make the acronym work, ha!) Sexuality, sensuality, sex, orgasms and love dynamics.

W= Work How fulfilled you are in your career or your entrepreneurial pursuits.

E= Environment Your home, travel, hobbies, social engagements, spaces and FUN time.

R = Relationships All your interpersonal relationships outside of romantic love, e.g. your family, friends, colleagues – and yourself.

As you can see, only *one* zone of the wheel relates to work, and yet it's what comes up time and time again in my work with clients and even my conversations with friends. Interestingly, 'Ooh' is always the last thing on everyone's lists – it seems to me that we're often sacrificing our own sensuality to focus on what we perceive to be society's measure of success. This is something I am fierce about transforming because it's something I've spent a lot of time working on myself. We can have great careers *and* great love lives and great sex. It's not a compromise.

I'd invite you now to construct a vision statement for each section of your Wheel of Possibility and include the values you've identified as your own. This is a mini paragraph on your desires for a particular area of your life, but you write the statement in the present tense as if it's already happening and add in your core values. Make sure you include how it would feel to live this as your reality.

Here's an example from Nicola, who is manifesting her entrepreneurial vision using tapping:

CASE STUDY: NICOLA'S VISION STATEMENT FOR HER WORK ZONE

I have a six-figure sustainable fashion business, which is sold at Selfridges, and I am recognised for the contribution it makes to society. I'm happily making a name for myself in an industry that I am passionate about and I care about going to work each day. I am looking for investment but I know that this will happen for me. I'm excited to expand my team and lead with empowered elegance.

This statement includes all Nicola's values, her energy, her unadulterated desires – and it's got a vibe about it, hasn't it? It's not wishful or hopeful, it's not task-orientated or fantastical – it feels grounded. Now it's your turn to create vision statements for each zone of the wheel. Once you've done this you can create a larger vision manifesto that encompasses each of the seven zones. This will also be in the present tense, but is the story of your future self. You can even create a visual mood board (vision board) of what this would look and feel like to you.

Now you know what you are aiming for, you can break it down and start tapping into each zone, noticing what you want to clear in order to create.

FOCUS ON THE FOCUS

I'm very intuitively systematic about where I place my focus and energy at any given time. When it comes to which area of the wheel you'd like to focus on, you're allowed to guess. Guessing is a playful way to tune in to your intuition more. I love making decisions quickly from a place that says, 'Yes, this sort of *feels* like it's time for me to create a more holistic wholeness by focusing on this *one* area of my life right now.' It pays off because it starts us off.

Last year, for example, I decided to strategically work on my Ooh zone, and although it was love and sex that were my primary focus, I noticed massive growth in other aspects of my life too, such as my finances. Does this seem surprising? Well, it shouldn't, because love, sex and money are connected energetically. Because my frequency was raised in my Ooh zone, the positive potential mirrored and expanded out to my income potential. Will I focus on money again as a primary desire? Yes, when the time feels right, but for now, I'm keeping my eyes on something else. Now I'm onto the Physical zone because I want to be more active and flexible (kind of due to the up-level in the sex life – it's all interconnected!).

The ultimate aim for every zone is to edge closer to 100 per cent over time, to pivot into your fullest power in each area of your life so that your Wheel of Possibility continues to expand. Check in every ninety days to see if you're ready to move on to another zone. Where your focus goes, your energy flows and your results pick up. You'll see subtle results and your self-belief will rise too. But if we try to do too much at once or 'have it all' in one quantum leap, we're setting ourselves up to let all these negative inner gremlins have their say at once. That's a horror movie I'd rather pass on, thanks.

I mentioned my client Farah Nazeer in the previous chapter. Well, she's a big fan of the wheel. It's been an important tool to help her organise both her tapping and her life, since it's allowed her to arrange what she calls 'the overwhelming nebulous mass'. As a result of this focused approach to her tapping and coaching work, she's much more able to see the bigger picture and create integration in her life so she can get on and kick ass changing the world.

MULTI-TASKING IS A CON

Energy must be directed. Think about your life for a minute and note down your big wins. Now cast your mind back and try to remember what you focused on *just* before that win. Did you divide your attention between twenty-five different things and everything just 'happened' to fall into place, or did you funnel your energy and willpower into specific and strategic success? Even if you think you're a fabulous multi-tasker (like I do), if we let our focus splay out like Bambi on the ice, we're actually just 'pissing in the wind', as my mum would say.

HACK: What we choose to focus on expands, which helped me to realise that all my successes in life were a result of focus. But so were my rubbish results. Are you able to give something undivided attention, and act strategically, according to your intuition? This may mean saying no to people and situations when they feel 'off'.

Multi-tasking in general is a con and if you think you're an expert life-juggler (like I do), then you are apparently in the 2 per cent of the population who get decent results from it. But studies show that it's not an effective approach to getting things done. A 2015 study carried out by academics at the University of Connecticut found that university students who tried to multi-task while doing their assignments took longer to complete their work and received overall lower grades than their peers. Similarly, a 2019 study by Stanford psychologists found that those of us who like to 'media multi-task' – listening to music or podcasts while checking emails or scrolling through Twitter while watching a film – find it more difficult to focus even when just carrying out one task.

What we *presume* to be doing many tasks at once is just lots of stops and starts. Our brain chooses what information to process at any given moment and if we don't get control over what that is, we get fuzzy and foggy.

What I have previously considered to be spinning plates like a badge of honour is actually trying to pretend that my brain works in a way it doesn't. Then I find myself in a cycle of getting angry with myself when I drop a plate. Grrrr, Poppy – you let it slip! As if I could feasibly keep up with my own sky-high expectations of myself. To give you some sense of my own embarrassing overloading, I moved house, put my son through university applications, wrote this book and ran my companies all during the same month and nearly tapped a dent in my forehead because I was so stacked up with multiple tasks. I think, 'Ah, I can do it!' But there's a limit. I didn't spot the clues that my body was giving me and my health suffered as a result. My output of energy and attention was scattered and fractured, and not enough of it was focused on my inner world: my biggest and most epic task. Sound familiar? We all do better with simplicity.

Dr Paul Atchley, an associate professor of cognitive psychology, tells us that:

'Based on over a half-century of cognitive science and more recent studies on multi-tasking, we know that multi-taskers do less and miss information. It takes time (an average of fifteen minutes) to re-orient to a primary task after a distraction such as an email. Efficiency can drop by as much as 40 per cent.'

Ouch. From the micro to the macro, for your own sake, and the sake of your end results, do less but do it with more focus.

So what to choose? I would suggest starting with a zone from the wheel like 'Work' or 'Money' or 'Environment' and devote attention to it by tapping on it repeatedly. Remember that *all* tapping is forward momentum towards your vision, and then the vision after that, and the one after that as they start to become your reality more and more quickly. The key to rapid effective manifestation is simply to focus, one step at a time, on what you want, while clearing energetic discord as you go within your belief system.

In bestselling author and associate professor of computer science Cal Newport's book, *Deep Work*, he explains that focusing on one thing well, which he calls 'the deep life', is the key to success but that it's often seen as paradoxical:

> *'The deep life, of course, is not for everybody. It requires hard work and drastic changes to our habits. For many, there's a comfort in the artificial busyness of rapid email messaging and social media posturing, while the deep life demands you leave much of that behind. There's also an uneasiness that surrounds any effort to produce the best things you're capable of producing, as this forces you to confront the possibility that your best life is not (yet) that good. It's safer to comment on our culture than to step into the Rooseveltian ring and attempt to wrestle it into something better.'*

But my spiritual mentor, my dad, once said to me the creative process begins with the mustard seed, it's actualised by depth and made manifest by a nurturing focus – we cannot be shallow. Neither can we be scattergun, impatient or blindsided by the huge swathes of people telling us it's not worth it. It *is* worth it. *You* are worth it. The effect you will have on the collective energy *will* be worth it.

We need courage when creating. Courage to stay in the vision and activate moments of 'flow state' where we are really involved and participating in whatever we are doing so 'something else' takes over. When your kids interrupt you or you have a million things to do . . . your mind is on something else: be careful it's not subconscious sabotage. Consciously, what can you do to create the environment you require? That creative space where we lose track of time and we access superconsciousness; infinite intelligence, way beyond our egocentric selves. We can top up this deeply productive time with rapid taps to keep our positive energy – so go for it, and don't be patchy with it. If in doubt, remember that you are always playing a matching game – does the frequency of what you want match the energy held in your belief system about it? Or is there a disconnect? You're looking to feel the warm possibility. Find that, feel that often – and you're rapidly accelerating towards creating your life desires.

ENGAGING WITH THE CURRENT SCENERY IN YOUR LIFE TO CREATE THE FUTURE

Holding a vision requires trust and patience so we don't get distracted by thoughts of what might go wrong within our own control systems and timelines. On the way to any destination there's always the scenery. Sometimes it's nice, like a pretty village, sometimes it's pretty dreary, like a building site, but it's all part of the route you've chosen to where you want to be. If we tap more often, we tend to be more relaxed, and because we've moved into our parasympathetic nervous system (the chilled response), our hearts can just take it all in.

'Life moves pretty fast. If you don't stop and look around once in a while, you could miss it.'
Ferris Bueller's Day Off (film)

Is it possible then, that with continued use of tapping – in all parts of the Wheel – you could look around to acknowledge, deeply and with heartfelt gratitude, the scenery of your life that is, in fact, the inevitable expression of your creative potential right now?

Your unique scenery exists to signpost your destination, but while we keep an eye on our goal, it's important not to be so blinded by the future that we don't notice the relevance of what is around us on the way.

All vision manifestation starts – and is sustained – with appreciation and gratitude for what we have now. We have so much, we are so very privileged. Eyes on the prize and all that, but to make it happen it's also about being in the little moments and using every moment as an opportunity for a frequency boost. If you don't already keep one, consider putting together a gratitude list: an ongoing high-vibrational list of things you feel grateful for (you can supercharge it with my simple Tapping into Gratitude exercise). It may seem like a small thing, but it has a huge effect on how you view your days. Lewis Howes, host of the incredibly popular podcast *School of Greatness*, says this about gratitude:

> '*Gratitude matters most. It's one of the core themes shared by all of the guests who come on the show. These are some of the most successful people on the planet. They can be, do, and have anything they want, and every single one of them is quick to talk about gratitude.*'

Exercise: Tapping into Gratitude

Make a list of every moment that is worth celebrating or appreciating during the day. An example list might look something like this:

- I am grateful for my morning coffee
- I appreciate my weekly book club

- I am so happy to be able to pick up ingredients for my favourite meal
- I am incredibly thankful for my inspiring friendship with Stella

Now jot down each thing that you're thankful for on individual slips of paper and place them in a glass jar. This is your gratitude jar. Whenever you feel negative emotions coming over you and you want to avoid spiralling, pick out a piece of paper from the jar and recall the memory written on it as you tap through the Rapid Tapping points. This will allow you to experience again the warm feelings of gratitude associated with the memory and help to improve your mood.

It's hard to be angry, resentful, upset *and* grateful at the same time. This is, quite paradoxically, the secret energy of creative transformation. The vision is coming, if you can courageously trust that it's on its way, and nurturing an attitude of gratitude, together with alleviating your stress levels, will allow you to do that. Less stress also equals more intuition. More intuition means you can hear your heart and simply *be*.

Here's an exercise to be more in the now, awaken your intuition and actively seek out the scenery in your own life.

Exercise: Awakening Intuition

This exercise is particularly useful if:

- You are not sure you can meditate

- You're not sure of the difference between your intuitive voice and your inner critic
- You want to soothe yourself before a journalling or visualisation
- You want to clear your mind from daily 'chatter'
- If you're too much in the past and stuck in a story about your life
- If you're too far in the future and dreaming rather than doing
- You want to be in the attitude of gratitude before you tap.

1 Look around the room or space you are in, let your gaze settle on something and stare at it. See if you can notice its intricacies, textures, colours, shapes.
2 Now, close your eyes.
3 Place your hands, one on top of the other, over your heart.
4 Take a few deep breaths in through your nose and out through your mouth. Practise conscious breathing. Take as long as you need here.
5 Notice your feet touching the surface beneath you, supporting you.
6 Feel your fingers and hands, wiggle them about and touch your skin. Sense the energy buzzing within them. Then, repeatedly tap the pad of your thumb on the pad of each finger. This is known as finger tapping and can be done simultaneously on both hands.
7 Try to notice your body and the way it feels. Scan your body from your feet to the crown of your head, and try to really feel the energy coming from the bottom to the

top of your being, pushing it upwards, through your heart to your head.

8 Consider all the many complicated rhythms going on beneath your skin, all the way down to your nerve endings and cells. Don't rush this: be grateful that your body can operate on your behalf in such a wonderful way.

9 Hear the sounds around you. Let them be, let them pass by.

10 Now listen for the silence too. There is always some silence around you, amidst the noise. Focus on this quiet space.

11 Accept everything as it is now by tapping on your collarbones and heart area saying, 'It is what it is.' The present moment is exactly what it is. Surrender to the present moment.

12 Now observe your mind: what's it doing? Wait for your next thought. If it pops up, let it pass and focus back on to your breath again, tapping on your collarbones and heart.

13 Now say aloud, 'I appreciate myself.'

14 Now say out loud, like counting sheep, all the many things you can be appreciative of.

15 Breathe in through your nose, hold for three seconds, and exhale out through your mouth as a sigh.

16 Be still and smile.

17 Now listen for a message. Your intuition will lead you to an image, a symbol, some words. Whatever it is be open and accept it. You can trust it. Receive it.

I don't need to tell you but it's vital to be mindful and make time for moments like this each day. I don't call this mindfulness so much as 'nowness', because it's not just about the mind, it's about your energy, your heart and your soul too; true appreciation of self and everything so you can awaken your highest levels of intuition. One of my favourite metaphysical teachers of all time is Eckhart Tolle, who wrote *The Power of Now* and *A New Earth*. If you want to go deeper into this area, I would suggest reading both titles.

HACK: When you are manifesting something, stop fretting about whether you're going to 'get it' or not. Assume you will, and affirm this belief over and over again. Notice every little bit of positive news to signal it's coming. Listen to your intuition not your logic. This is where the magic moments of the present collect, like little pebbles of superconscious energy, amassing into a tidal wave of loving reciprocity just for you.

PERSIST UNTIL YOU NO LONGER RESIST

How often do you resist something rather than receive it? From intuition to manifestations, we can avoid the very thing we dearly want. The well-known Jungian understanding of 'what we resist persists' – which means each time we avoid something it comes back stronger – can also be used in reverse. If we persist with our tapping and our heartfelt goals it means we can also help shortcut our manifestations by ironing out any resistance with a degree of persistence.

It's not enough to wait for the bus, but then choose to give up if three minutes have passed and it hasn't turned up. It won't work if you walk away.

One of my clients, Wizz Selvey, ex-head of beauty buying at Selfridges for over a decade and now known as the 'Queen of Retail', is a woman who's constantly busy – but she makes time for tapping each day. At first, she underestimated how much happiness it could bring her. To inspire you, she says this of her new ability to persist with her tapping regime:

'Rapid Tapping has become a priority in my life, the speed of change I see in my mood, mindset and energy is so quick. It started as a way to clear negative beliefs, patterns and blocks, which I often was not aware of, but as I've done it more with Poppy it has developed into a feeling of euphoria and a sense that anything is possible. I regularly use the Rapid Tapping routines and now have the confidence to do it myself on the go too, which can have enormous benefits.'

Like Wizz, don't overthink it: just do it. Little and often. It's more about persistence within the moment to see, feel and believe than obsessing over the culturally conditioned inability within us to fail. We might well fail, fail fast and start again, because that's not the problem here. The only problem is not bouncing back again so the worries win – don't let those bastards bring you down.

In his book *Bliss Brain*, Dawson Church offers an effective four-stage meditation process to access a state called 'bliss brain':

*'Focus is when attention is centred in the meditative state.
Then Mind Wandering Begins. We become Aware that the
mind is wandering, then Shift ourselves back into focus.'*

I like the idea of it all being a cycle. We are continually pivoting
and shifting; we just need to accept that it is what it is, and go
back to what we're dreaming of. If we don't, we compromise on
the vision and we compensate for not having it (usually by avoid-
ance or self-indulgent behaviours). Keep the creative tension there
because it's all just a big cycle of bouncing back again.

You're resilient. Get back up. Who made it wrong to fail? You
started doing this when you were a toddler. Fall, cry, let it go, make
it happen by trying again. Don't stop now, and don't stop your
tapping process either. Feeling wobbly and making mistakes is a
natural and expected part of evolution.

NEGATIVE VISIONING: HOW TO MAXIMISE YOUR MANIFESTING

A word of warning: you are likely to have a negative, or restricting,
vision for your life. But you don't want to create a vision based on
what you don't want. It's not meant to come from an energy of
escapism or fantasy, since you create based on how you feel. If you
approach your vision from a place of held pain, and you're focused
on avoiding your past or your present life, it's not as freeing or
expansive as it could be. I see many people underplay what they
could go for because of this unseen energetic attachment. Without
tapping to clear unhelpful beliefs, you may be trying to achieve
things based on a vibration of fixing yourself. Of trying to patch

up holes in your self-worth bucket. Also if you want something just to get back at someone, to prove you're better than someone or to 'shove it to the man', this isn't a good foundational vision vibe. That's why creating a clear, positive vision (with or without a vision board) and forgetting to use tapping afterwards is a self-defeating, slower decision.

So let's lay it all out on the table. Are you ready to get closer to making your vision a reality? Good, because the clearing work is about to begin!

5 CLEARING THE PATH

It's time to clear the bridge of objections, excuses and blocks on your pathway to joy, everything that's holding you back – clear that shit out. Let's get serious and real about the stuff we no longer want to deal with. We all have traumatic experiences and accompanying emotions from which we want to free ourselves, from relationship woes to money mindset issues to a lack of confidence. Whatever you feel you've gone through so far in life, it's time to give yourself a permanent permission slip to finally overcome it and leave it where it belongs: in the past. You can rewrite the story of your life from today . . . life is *now*.

What I refer to as clearing work can occur on both 'macro' and 'micro' levels (which we will call 'deep' and 'daily'). Macro-clearing is deep tapping, where we focus on using tapping to undo some of the bigger, more entrenched traumas and stresses that have uniquely plagued us throughout our lives. For this kind of work, I would recommend an EFT tapping session as it allows you to go very deep into an issue with a skilled practitioner, who can hold you and support you as you fight emotional demons.

Rapid Tapping, on the other hand, lends itself well to themes you want to create more of in your life such as unshakeable confidence, improved relationships, positive vibes and more. It also helps to quieten the negative chatter in your mind and is perfect for what I call SOS micro-clearing (rebalancing 'help me!' moments in your day), which is less confronting work and speedier to do. That said, in this chapter, I'm particularly targeting any unsavoury past 'stuff'.

Many EFT therapists and psychologists define trauma as falling into two categories: big T trauma and little t trauma. Here's a nuts and bolts definition: 't' traumas are things that happen that we aren't able to cope with in the moment and that cause a disruption in our emotional functioning. These are events that leave us feeling helpless but aren't inherently life-threatening. 'T' trauma generally refers to an extremely significant event that leaves you feeling powerless and unable to fight back.

Trauma affects us all differently, and I've been through my fair share: my dad's slow and debilitating cancer, my own battles with skin cancer, my divorce and parenting as a single, working mum. But I don't consider these to be big T for me. For me big T would have been an experience of being locked in a room with a dog barking (difficult to understand for those who love dogs) before tapping helped me get over my phobia. Big T for you could be having to move home, being made redundant, or maybe something more horrific that's masquerading as small t. I've had friends pulling 'stay-at-home-and-cry' sickies about a bad paint job of their office (true story) and some who have taken a bullet to the heart from a cheating partner as if it's a bad day at the office. We are all different. The jury is out and not really important on this one. The most important thing is to remember that the emotional attachments are created like a kaleidoscopic snapshot of the *moment* the trauma sets in — and then later reinforced. Aspects remembered that are related to the experience will pop up to give us a blurred perspective sometimes too.

What has happened before contributes to the experience of the now. The funny thing is that all experience is neutral at the core – and we can establish a level playing field very quickly if we treat all these memories with tapping next time they pop up.

This kind of triggering – much like going to a therapist to discuss something horrible – can feel a bit scary, so use this simple and calming exercise to help.

Tapping exercise: My Mindfulness Tap

1 Take a deep breath in through your nose and exhale through your mouth.
2 Start tapping on your collarbones and heart area.
3 With eyes open, look in detail at everything around you right now and notice each part of what you see.
4 Sense the sound, the shape, the temperature of the air on your skin, breathing mindfully and consciously as you do this.
5 Now home in on something in your eyeline, and focus on it for a couple of minutes.
6 Take a deep breath in through your nose and exhale out through your mouth.
7 Relax and be still.

Notice how the experience of just being present in the moment is completely neutral; our own perspective is what creates the emotional attachment to it. Tapping doesn't change memories or experiences; it just tweaks the feeling we create around them and the meaning we assign to them.

> **HACK:** Don't underestimate the importance of
> working on dissipating the micro or daily stresses
> that have a significant and cumulative impact on our
> lives. Left unattended, without a quick tap, these SOS
> moments (I feel sick, I can't do it, I'm too tired, I'm
> too busy) turn into micro beliefs, which hook in and
> affect our decisions negatively.

Just like we begin at the root with deep clearing and move to the positives created with the daily work, each individual tap also moves through the two-part process of clearing and creating, beginning with the clearing of old evidence and moving to the creating of new evidence once we are able to accept the energy shifts more wholly.

Let's look at a real example here. A client of mine, Claudia Stebbings, is a highly talented and accomplished global marketing leader but was nervous about taking a leap into a role outside her previous remit within news. She struggled in interviews for roles she was perfectly suited to. Held back by her gremlins, she convinced herself that the reason she felt this way was because she wasn't good enough.

To try to combat this, Claudia was using positive affirmations daily but they weren't working. So instead I encouraged her to use Rapid Tapping to tap on the themes of self-doubt, self-love and resistance to communicate to her nervous system that the value of new experience – whether good or bad – is that it expands your evidence base. She finally accepted that it was the fear of something potentially going wrong in a new industry that was really holding her back. She hadn't realised that failure can be a necessary part of the growth process and not something to shy away from. End result? She went for – and was offered – her dream role in the wine industry, something we had put onto her vision manifesto and tapped on!

Now tap with me on your collarbones and heart area as you say this affirmation:

Possibility exists in all new experiences.

And this one:

It is safe for me to accept new experiences because I am gathering new evidence.

As well as creating new experiences as much as possible, we can also actively and rigorously tap daily on reducing the weight of the old evidence. Each tap helps to raise your frequency and magnetism so you can sit with the unknown more easily.

My clients and I make this part of the process ultra-effective by tracking tapping over a period of time – a week, a month, six months, a year – it doesn't matter. Just pick a timeline to start with.

TRACKING YOUR TAPS OVER TIME

A note here if you're ever feeling any guilt about shining brightly and being happy. There's nothing wrong with wanting the best for yourself and others. Unleashing your potential is why we tap! You know we are not here on this planet to *cope*. We are designed to be a joyful part of a massive and ever-expanding universe – I don't love the idea that we have to just survive our way through it, pay our bills and die. Only using tapping for clearing away the negatives is like continually cleaning your house but not bothering to put any furniture in it, or invite any guests inside. Say no to a 'meh' life. If you shine, others can too. Brighten up someone's day after a tap, by sharing this work with them.

As well as for individual taps, you can apply the Frequency Finder Scale (see below) to your tapping stats over weeks and months, which will give you a useful insight into your own emotional state and how it's improving. Make tapping a part of your lifestyle and track your upward progress over time. Making your practice a daily habit need not be hard. If you keep an eye on the fast and long-lasting benefits of tapping, you will easily create the habit – and, what's more, Rapid Tapping is, well, very *rapid*.

To start a habit successfully we need to:

- See the positive effects becoming real evidence over time
- See what we are aiming for (the overall vision)

To give yourself a leg-up, you can track your taps to tangibly see how your baseline frequency changes for the better. This is often the big shocker for those who work with me privately, because, over time, subtle shifts add up: every tap you take is not just alleviating a certain specific issue (for example anxiety over public speaking), but is also contributing to the upward spiral of your entire vibration. Waking up noticing that you've started each tap higher up the scale is a wonderful acknowledgement that your daily dose is working in a 360° way.

You will also start to gain awareness of your most dominant emotions or 'feels', as I call them, over time. You'll start to sense how you often struggle with certain emotions, like guilt or shame or anger. You'll also notice how much better you feel after a tap, calm or light or happy. I call this a *pre-* and *post*-tap emotion, and I like to take a photo of my face before and after too. I think an improved emotional or mental state really shows in the face.

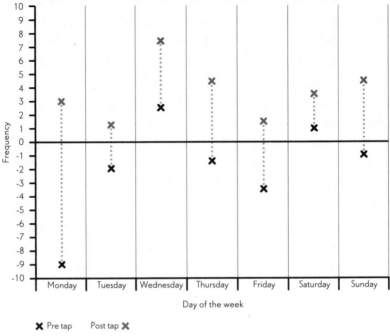

The Frequency Finder Scale

This scale is not an exact science, but is a way to keep track of your emotional responses and growth week by week, and where they tend to show up within your personal frequency.

Your intention is to raise your frequency over time. This is entirely possible for you. Taking note of our vibrational resonance – our energy – helps guide our tapping. For example, take Ben, a CFO and keen tapper. When Ben first started tapping through the routines, he often felt shame, guilt and self-doubt coming up. You often begin a tap at a low starting point, at -7 on the scale. Over time, Ben started to notice that he was starting his tapping at a +5 and the compounded *feeling* he began sealing in was tingly, light and happy – he used the simple scale to note his progress and add in the unique way he responded, and how his body also responded. It's very personal to you, because each frequency is different, a blueprint of your own unique energy code. The frequency scale is your navigation tool. Our feelings are not static, so some days will be low and some high, but you'll be less disheartened if you can sense an overall pattern of growth.

STAYING ABOVE THE LINE

Your baseline frequency – the overall sense of how you manifest day to day – is something we can shift by embodying emotions that lend themselves to what I like to call above-the-line living.

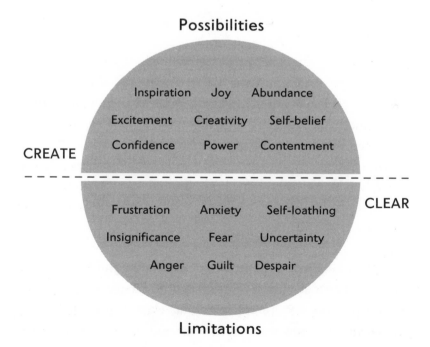

Possibilities

Inspiration   Joy   Abundance

Excitement   Creativity   Self-belief

CREATE   Confidence   Power   Contentment

- -

CLEAR   Frustration   Anxiety   Self-loathing

Insignificance   Fear   Uncertainty

Anger   Guilt   Despair

Limitations

If you've ever wondered why you're not getting what you want, it's most likely because you're experiencing below-the-line emotions.

When you track your taps or use the Frequency Scale, I'd love for you to become aware and accepting of whether your feelings are generally positive or negative. Of course, I'm not saying you can't be low, but being truly attuned to how you're feeling will allow you to avoid the negative spirals, lacklustre results and mis-informed actions. If I sense that I'm sinking below the line, I'll take action to change my day and this might be in the form of a gratitude exercise, a rapid tap or doing something I love. After all, feeling snazzy doesn't just happen, and you want to make sure you're positive and primed for manifesting.

RAPID DAILY CLEARING TAP

Use this if you are in a negative emotional state or somewhere between 0 and -10 on the frequency scale. You can also use this to clear any latent remaining imbalances even if you're feeling in a plus positive state (0 to +10) on the frequency scale.

> **HACK:** You can always upgrade your subconscious and you can't 'catch' negativity by saying it aloud.

Do this as part of your daily routine or when something particularly emotional triggers you, to help shift the energy at the time of the experience (for example, a colleague upsets you, something bad happens or you just feel a bit edgy).

Tapping exercise: Rapid Daily Clearing Tap

1   Where are you on the frequency scale from -10 to +10?
    Write down your score or say it aloud to track it.
2   Breathe in a long deep breath through your nose, and
    exhale as a sigh; repeat a few times.

Next, sore spots massage and the three-step routine:

I feel ...
(say your own truthful emotion or feeling)

Because ...
*(add your reasoning, what's making you feel this way –
quickly add your answer and don't overthink it, try to let
your intuition guide you)*

**But/And I choose to acknowledge and accept this is the
way it is right now.**

3   Tap the Rapid Points as you use these releasing
    affirmations:

- I choose to release my negative emotions as much as I
  can, right now
- I am willing to love myself regardless of these feelings
- It is possible for me to release these emotional
  attachments.

4   Tap the points as you focus on where this might be holding emotional tension in your body:

- I can feel it in my body
- All this tension in my body here (you can place or hover one hand above where the pain is)
- I'm grateful that my body knows what to do
- But I reduce the tension in my body now
- I choose to release the tension
- It is possible for me to be calm and centred.

5   Keep tapping as you repeat these affirmations and focus on the feelings until you notice a shift, a bit of a bodily change somehow, or like it's just time to stop.
6   Finish with a check in on your Frequency Finder Scale (are you feeling the same or better?)
7   Take a deep inhalation through your nose and exhale through your mouth to calibrate your new energy and seal it in.
8   Affirm this aloud:

It is possible for me to be calm and centred.

Once you become familiar with all the taps in this book, you can decide which feel appropriate for a given day. If you're feeling fabulous, reach for one of the rapid taps in the create part of the book (Part Two). If you're feeling a bit low, perhaps start with this tap and then choose another tap from this clearing section.

UNDERSTANDING THE MIND–BODY CONNECTION

The 'mind–body' is one entity, says bestselling author and professor of family medicine and public health Deepak Chopra. Rapid Tapping uses this theory as a core pillar. There is a synergy that exists between our mind and our body, so although we look at both individually throughout this book we assume that they operate as one.

One way to connect to your creative self when manifesting is to connect to your body just before you go to sleep; at this point your mind is all over the place, but your subconscious is just revving up for continuous 24/7 downloads throughout the night. What you focus on before you sleep really matters, so we want to gently clear away as much 'junk' as we can before we slumber. It's like brushing your teeth – add it to your nightly hygiene routine.

A powerful sleep tap is described here:

Tapping exercise: The Sleep Tap

1 Start by either dimming your lights or switching them off altogether.
2 Play tranquil soothing music like solfeggio tones or relaxing meditation music, perhaps some sound bowls – whatever works well for you.

SAY IT **I am feeling content, sleepy and full of love.**

Say this affirmation out loud.

SCORE IT How possible is this feeling as a percentage?

CLEAR IT Sore spots massage:

- I feel like I can't switch off right now
- Because I have thoughts in my head
- But I choose to accept that right now
- It's just my mind trying to keep me safe.

Focus on the thoughts that want to be heard, racing through your mind. Tap through the Rapid Tapping points, breathing deeply as you go, settling on your collarbones and heart area when you feel calmer and sleepier.

- All of these thoughts and feelings from the day
- I choose to let them release into love.

Now let your mind take you to something you love: a person, a pet, a beautiful visual or the sound of waves on the beach. Whatever brings you into love.

CREATE IT Keep tapping on your collarbones and heart area as you say:

- I can relax now
- I am returning to love
- It is possible for me to see love instead of fear now
- I sleep soundly
- I am manifesting as I sleep
- All is well.

SEAL IT Now relax and tap on your fingertips gently as you repeat this affirmation, beginning with your decision. Seal it in before you fall asleep:

I decide to feel content, sleepy and full of love
I am feeling content, sleepy and full of love
I am feeling content, sleepy and full of love.

WHO'S AFRAID OF THE BIG BAD FEAR?

We all are. We have all walked this earth. Sometimes, when working with clients, I've found that it's a lack of love that leads to an influx of fear, and often that's a cue for me to get them to tap into self-love instead. Love starts with us. I have also found that the fear often comes from a fear of fear itself. We are scared to feel fear. We pretend we are strong, unafraid. Women, for example, are often afraid to show any sign of weakness for fear that they will be seen as damsels in distress, and not the strong, independent women that they are.

Well, hands up. I feel fear. I've also feared the idea of being a wimpy woman. I don't want to be one of *them* – no way, I am no victim. I am independent. I can do this and I am not afraid. Familiar rhetoric? Yep, I imagine so.

Fear is unavoidable. We have to feel it when we're experiencing something unfamiliar but we don't have to feel it when we are going over old ground because that's not helping us grow. In either case, I learned through Marianne Williamson that if we gravitate back to love we are then connecting with the innate energy field, rather than a learned behaviour.

*'Love is what we were born with. Fear is what we
learned here.'*

MARIANNE WILLIAMSON, author

Remember, if you've learned something, it is possible for
you to unlearn it. So if you're feeling anxiety and fear, use this
routine each day for seven days and notice how you're coming
back to love:

Tapping exercise: The 'Moving Past Fear' Tap

This may feel uncomfortable or confronting, so make
sure that you are in a safe space and feeling prepared
to embark on this tap. Once you are ready, bring your
fears to mind with intent for a minute, quietly. Notice
where you are on the frequency scale from −10 to
+10. Intend to raise your frequency and move past the
grip of fear.

SORE SPOTS MASSAGE

- I feel all this fear because ... *(say your intuitive answer
  quickly here)*
- And it makes me feel ...
- But I'm willing to love myself anyway
- I am scared on some level, I'm willing to love and
  accept myself
- My fear is my resistance and it's scary
- But it's OK

- I'm choosing to move towards love anyway
- It is possible for me to choose love now.

CLEAR IT Tap through the Rapid Tapping points, one for each statement:

- All this fear
- I feel it
- All this fear
- All this fear
- Fear
- My fear
- All this fear
- Fear

Take a breath, inhale through your nose, exhale out through your mouth:

- I choose to release this fear right now
- Even if I don't know how
- Maybe on some level I don't want to release this fear
- I know this fear quite well now
- What would it mean if I didn't have this fear
- What would I have to be like if I didn't have this fear?
- That's scary too
- I can feel this fear
- And that's OK right now
- My body recognises this fear
- My body is keeping me safe
- But what if I didn't have to be afraid any more?
- I'm giving myself permission to release the fear

- And be calmer
- Because it's stressful being alive
- And it's scary as well
- And I accept that now.

Take a breath, inhale through your nose, exhale out through your mouth:

- Even though I have this feeling right now
- I love and accept this is the way it is right now
- Even though I have this current feeling in my body
- That's OK because I'm noticing it right now
- Even though I have this feeling right now and I'm becoming familiar with that ...
- I choose to accept myself for who I am now
- All this remaining fear
- When I think about my life
- Or my work
- I choose to let go of
- I'm choosing to release the fear now
- I'm choosing to believe I am enough as I am now
- Because I'm a human being
- And I am OK even with some fear
- But I'm choosing a better thought wherever I can.

Take a breath, inhale through your nose, exhale out through your mouth. Notice where in your body you still feel this fear.

- I feel it in my body here ... *(focus on it; you can also place or hover your hand over the area)*

- I feel this discomfort now
- All this tension
- I can feel it in my body here ...
- I know my mind is connected to my body
- And I'm so grateful that I have a body that responds to me
- Trying to keep me safe
- But what if I could communicate to release some fear?
- Yes I can do that
- I'm choosing to work with my body right now
- I release myself back into harmony and love.

AFFIRM IT Take a breath, smile and tap on your collarbones and heart area.

I am choosing to focus on love
I am choosing love
I choose love.

Take a breath and stretch out, move and shake out your hands.

Now try to bring back the same level of fear as you had before. It should be harder to feel as much fear.

You're returning to love. Feels lovely doesn't it?

6 SHIFTING INTO NEW POSSIBILITIES

Are you ready to slip into a deeper ocean of positive energy? It's time to create key habits, so grab your pen and journal as we get ready to start creating. One thing to remember now is to be ultra-conscious about the dwelling state you're mostly in. Remember the Flow of Life? Remember how your thoughts can't all be controlled, yet your frequency can be?

Something that helped me come up with the name for my members club, House of Possibility (a self-development home for pioneering thinkers and seekers), is this beautiful poem by the great Emily Dickinson. I believe, metaphorically, that it shows the beauty of what is possible for us if we intend to dwell in positive energetic resonance.

I dwell in Possibility – (466)
EMILY DICKINSON

I dwell in Possibility –
A fairer House than Prose –
More numerous of Windows –
Superior – for Doors –

Of Chambers as the Cedars –
Impregnable of eye –
And for an everlasting Roof
The Gambrels of the Sky –

Of Visitors – the fairest –
For Occupation – This –
The spreading wide my narrow Hands
To gather Paradise –

Tapping is not just a solution from struggle. It's a springboard towards our own personal paradise, and now that you've shifted closer to that paradise land, it's time to double down on releasing all the old patterns that still trigger emotional imbalance and energetic friction. Keep a list up your sleeve of what's repeatedly bothering you as you go about your day-to-day life.

Here's a few I keep an eye on. Which of these do you need to tap on too?

- Releasing my control over a tightly organised life and perfectionism (yawn)
- Releasing my resistance to my own success (how big will I let this become?)
- Releasing blame (thou shalt not throw the first stone and all that!)
- Releasing my fear of what might happen if . . . (cue the long list of presumptions)
- Releasing my 'fiercely independent' tendencies (I'm fine, thanks very much)
- Releasing the urge to procrastinate (hmmm, that light needs fixing)

- Releasing the negative self-talk (hello gremlins, welcome back. Oh – you never left)

It's a good time to remember why we're doing all this releasing stuff again, and there are two reasons: firstly, to tap into our true power and potential as superconscious and attuned beings living out our envisioned life; and, secondly, to ease up on ourselves for being in a fragile, egotistical vessel governed by brain activity that's trying to keep us safe from harm.

In a nutshell: our soul wants us to fly, but our body wants us to settle.

'I am a cage in search of a bird.'

FRANZ KAFKA

Refuse to settle! Life can throw all sorts at us, and just when we think we're getting ready to fly to a future of freedom, we realise our old cage is still there, dragging us back indoors. Some of us feel hemmed in by a metaphorical cage; others feel as rusty and fixed as an actual one. Maybe you observe life from that alluring bird's-eye view? Or maybe you feel like a dead bird on someone's Christmas dinner table. Whatever shape you're in, you *can* live an uncaged life. Hallelujah.

To live an uncaged life is to unashamedly combat our bodily instinct to settle in the past and to move it very mindfully into the future – and to be OK with what is happening in the present moment. The more we make peace with the negative energy of the past, the less we carry that same energy into our envisioned life. To be fully free and content is a complete acceptance of 'what is', even if you don't like it. Accepting what is without resistance or obsessively controlling the 'how' (hands up if you're always straight to the 'so how do I do that?' spiel) is the first step towards true emotional freedom and a leap in the direction of effective manifesting. But it's hard to focus on the possibilities when you feel caged in by the day-to-day triggers. Let's free ourselves from our cages so we can be wild.

USING A TRIGGER LIST

It is what it is.
Try saying these words aloud now and sense how your energy reacts. If you're anything like me, you're usually saying this in a passive-aggressive voice when your partner breaks something. Or when a friend spills a glass of wine all down your dress and your response is 'Oh, don't worry – it is what it is.' Inside you're seething 'moron!' – but on the surface you're all fine and dandy. This is exactly the kind of vibe we're addressing in this exercise.

Over the next few weeks you're going to watch yourself for all the crappy things you say, feel, think, and do as *reactions*. A reactive life is not a progressive, fully manifesting one. Be honest and list out all your trademark reactive responses. What reactions are you having to seemingly anodyne stuff, what day-to-day scenarios grind you down? What kind of people bug you? What memories pop up in your day and hassle you? What kind of thing throws you into your low vibration? Which daily activities or issues unleash your inner hell-raiser (and not in a good way)? What reactions and vices are you not proud of? What below-the-line emotions are always rising to the surface? Keep a note. You're playing detective here, remember.

In Rapid Tapping, we call these triggers: sneaky little reminders that take you back in time. Notice how they never trigger you forward? They're always going back to something you have marked with an energetic red flag. Perhaps you've considered your own triggers to be a character fault, but I see them as helpful clues. These are what you want to build up with glee, because if you direct your tapping onto them one by one, starting with the trigger that seems to come up a lot for you, or the ones that feel most raw . . . you're winning. You're knocking them out like that slightly sadistic kids' game 'Whack-a-mole'. Thwack.

Your list should look something like this:

- I forgot an appointment then cried because I never forget appointments. What is happening to me?!
- I got annoyed in that meeting and called Paul a twat in my head.
- I saw a bad photo of myself and felt instantly rubbish.
- I flew off the handle at Bob again.
- I went to the fridge and ate pizza again.
- I got really tired and moaned at my kids again.

Why use the trigger list?

This is really useful when you're wondering what to tap on. And super-handy if you start shifting into a realm of possibility and thinking, hmmm, where to go next? By referring back to your trigger list routinely, you can start clearing very specific, suppressed energy blocks, which will open up more space for positive energy.

Here is a quick 'go-to' tap, for when you're using your trigger list or looking to come to terms with 'what is' (and drop the pretence that you're 'fine') on any given day.

Tapping exercise: The 'It Is What It Is' Tap

SORE SPOTS MASSAGE

Right now, I feel ...
Because ...
But it is what it is.

Say this affirmation out loud.

CLEAR IT Tap through the Rapid Tapping points:

- I choose to accept this is the way I feel right now
- What a relief to say that out loud
- I choose to be kind to myself and others, no matter how I feel
- I do still feel ... *(insert any remaining negative emotions)*
- I choose to release any old emotional energy that's triggering me
- Right now
- What if it felt safe to feel better right now?
- Maybe it doesn't feel OK
- Maybe it does feel OK to let this go
- It's happened and I can't change that
- I still feel a bit ... *(express any lingering negative or limiting feelings)*
- But the energy doesn't need to stay with me
- I can let the emotional attachment go
- I can change my energy
- But I can unhook myself from any negative energy

- I powerfully choose that all I have is the present moment
- Because all I have is the now
- And the future
- The past is the past
- And my choice is to let the energy pass now
- It's safe for me to let the energy change
- And it is done.

Now take a stretch and inhale deeply. Notice how you may feel different, calmer, more at peace within the moment, which is magical. If you don't, repeat the sequence as many times as you need.

Shake it out, then continue with sealing in this new energy:

SEAL IT

- This is my new choice, I choose to feel ... *(insert positive feeling that you have felt a spark of already)*
- I'm willing to feel ...
- I'm willing to feel ...
- Because ... *(choose a benefit)*
- Because ...
- Because ...
- I choose to feel this way because ...
- Because ...
- So this is my powerful free choice and I'm leaning into this today
- I'm smiling into this today *(smile here!)*
- It is now more possible for me to feel ... *(insert your new positive feeling)*

Now take a stretch, smile and inhale deeply.

With the following steps remember you want to place more pressure when you tap and really GO FOR IT with belief! See if you can remember something funny, or spontaneously laugh.

AFFIRM IT March on the spot if you can as you thump your thymus three times with intention and conviction. As you do so, keep repeating:

It is possible for me to feel ...
It is possible for me to feel ...

Of course, sometimes this isn't enough and you need something stronger. Perhaps you've had a really difficult day. Then what? The tapping equivalent of a double whisky is coming up now for just those moments, my friend! The wonderful thing about tapping in a high emotional state is that you're literally allowing the energy to pass as it's meant to. When it comes to emotion, it's best to let it all hang out and transmute that energy immediately. If you do, you're cutting down any future additions to your trigger list, because there's less emotional attachment to an experience.

This next useful SOS rapid tap will quickly alleviate high stress and clear painful energy from a negative or shocking experience. In the heat of the moment it's not always easy to remember which tap to use, so this one is speedy and super-easy to recall. It will also help you deal with day-to-day frustrations. When someone triggers you, when something makes you want to spiral into a negative loop, when you're getting angry at your kids, this is a good tap to turn to. It won't take you longer than two minutes; if you want to delve deeper, you can tap for five minutes or choose a tap to follow up with.

Tapping exercise: The SOS Tap

Start by tapping only on your collarbones and heart area, and say the following:
(*Insert what's happened…*) **and it makes me feel …** (*insert your negative feeling*)

I feel it here in my body … (*focus on where you feel it in your body, like your stomach or in the chakras, if you like to use those*) **and it feels like** (*describe the way it feels in your body, like a tight knot or a stabbing pain or numbness*).

Inhale and exhale. Repeat, filling in the blanks and seeing what you notice.

HACK: For this particular rapid tap you don't need to ask *why* you feel something. Tapping is somatic – and remember, we are dealing with energy fields, not just complicated logic on a purely therapeutic basis. For other taps, I'll introduce a certain degree of self-enquiry with adding a *because*; for this one, it's just about the *what*.

YOU ARE INFINITE

I know I've said we're finite and we all die (keep the mood up, Poppy), but actually we are *infinite*; something on which so many of the most successful and content human beings on the planet seem to agree. It's a common view among many of the world's top movers and shakers.

If we are going to reframe our lives along these lines we need to understand that we can't access infinite possibilities until we accept that we are spiritual beings experiencing what it means to be human (and that our minds are limited). Humans fuck up. That's the way it's meant to be. Only then can each of us *really* tap into what we all ultimately want: to experience life in JOY.

Struggling with self-directed negativity is understandable, but I've decided that I'm not going to beat up my fragile ego any more, when it's just doing the best it can with the form it has here on this planet. I need to be compassionate. If I am cruel to myself, I'm simply kicking my soul in the teeth for being 'not enough'. How dare I do that?

All my own selfing and self-talk arises when I settle for a limited landscape of life. But when I'm tapped into something I can't possibly explain but that I can feel, I can access a higher level of contentment.

Want to get out of your own way? Thymus-thump your way to truly believing you are infinite. See if choosing to believe this statement brings you to a new level of peaceful love and kindness for yourself and everyone on the planet.

I am infinite. *(Thymus thump)*
I am infinite. *(Thymus thump)*
I am infinite. *(Thymus thump)*

I truly believed this growing up and my belief was solidified in me as my dad died in my arms when I was nineteen. In the hospital together, just us, I was connected to something unshakeably spiritual. As he took his last breath, I could see his soul moving on. He was eternal, infinite, magical . . . and I realised in that moment that we all are.

We are not our bodies. We are not even our feelings. We are so much more. If we are spiritually starved, perhaps pretending that we are not magical, badass beings helps fill up that void.

As bestselling metaphysical and inspirational author Dr Wayne Dyer said:

'Change the way you look at things, and the things you look at change.'

This kind of core change relies on constant doses of self-love. The more of that we have, the more we can manifest.

Self-love for the soul

So what is self-love? Self-love is when we acknowledge our emotions and validate our imperfections unconditionally, so there is nothing that detaches us from that feeling of being part of the infinite. Anything other than this definition will separate us from superconsciousness, which means we are relying only on our fragile human ego to get through life. It's no wonder then that we think we're not up to scratch. It's *only* through the human ego that we can meet experiences, traumas, big changes, people and scenarios that really pull that sense of unconditional love into question. We feel guilty, we don't trust ourselves or others, we feel unworthy or that we don't belong – and it's easy to fall into the trap of self-loathing (especially when you know what you now know about how the brain works and that we are a record of our past).

Here's a list of ten prompts that I learned from Dr Dyer's various texts that helped me get started on my own self-love for the soul journey:

1. Say 'I love all parts of myself' in the mirror when you feel down. A mirror affirmation allows you to form a connection to yourself. Supercharge this by tapping on your heart area.

2. 'I am whole and perfect as I was created.' Laminate it and be in the space with the words. You might also say, 'I am not my body or my achievements.'

3. Stop judging yourself and others; appreciate that you're part of the infinite and judgement can't even exist in it.

4. 'I belong here.' Your presence here has a purpose you're not aware of. You are meant to be occupying this space at this precious time in humanity – you're not here by accident.

5. You're never alone. Go and find someone who thinks they're alone and convince them that they're not (go and do that – then take your own advice).

6. Respect your body – honour the temple that houses you. Lay off the bad stuff.

7. Meditate more.

8. Make amends with adversaries. Radiating forgiveness helps get rid of hidden debilitating energy that gets in the way of manifesting.

9. Always remember the self in self-respect – the

opinions of others are not facts, neither are others' opinions facts for you (just take a look at social media).

10. Be an appreciator not a depreciator (choose gratitude not hopelessness).

Even though it may seem that you've expanded yourself as far as you can go in terms of what you can achieve, feel like, or become ... you haven't. The journey is about to get really magical now.

When it came to my love life, I recently made a fundamental decision to say *no* to society's metrics of how long things 'should' take or what is humanly possible for me, sexually. I did the clearing with tapping (lots of it – and that was painful and emotional, and I was surprised how much I still needed to do), but I also spent a lot of time creating the resonance I require to believe I can have this now – and fast. I met the love of my life by chance, and within six weeks we had decided to buy a home together. We put an offer in on a dream home (very much aligned to the vibe of my vision board) that four other people wanted – and we were chosen. They accepted the offer. I later learned they just 'felt' the energy was right and we were the ones and they couldn't explain why. The man I love matches, to the slightest of detail, *everything* I desired, deserved and knew was possible for me to attract into my life. My clients even call him the mysterious linen shirt man, because, as I mentioned earlier, a man who wears linen shirts was a specific detail I was looking for!

But I had to say 'hell, no' to a lot of mediocre assumptions about what is possible in order to get into the vibration to receive him. I had worked on the 'Ooh' area of the Wheel of Possibility before to help manifest partners, but it turns out those unions, although each beautiful in their own right, were prepping me to evolve and become an even higher vibration so I could be ready for *this* man. But, even when me and linen shirt man got together – and here come the fear goblins – I started thinking, this is too good to be true! What if something goes wrong? What if he dies? This is too soon! What if he leaves me? What if he turns out to be some sort of maniac?

I tapped into it and realised: I've manifested him for *right now* and this is *not* the frequency of gratitude or acceptance. I told myself that I had to focus on staying in the matching (joyful) frequency *now* and become more of the woman I want to be for him – and for myself. Kind, thoughtful, empowered, accomplished, caring, sexy, loving, happy, enthusiastic, adoring, silly. If he stays this way for me in return, then we are on an energetic level. If I catch myself delving into the 'What ifs?', I answer my own questions instead: What if . . . ? Well, what if *what*?

What if . . .?

Usually, we try to avoid or over-analyse or bury these niggling worries, but the goal in Rapid Tapping is to simply call them out and make them as preposterous as we can. Having worked in TV for decades, specialising in creating programmes with celebrities and comics and even writing for my own comedy panel shows, flirting with the funny is central to my work. It's also a technique to transform the psyche by directly challenging a psychological stance; in NLP when we challenge assumptions using deliberately oppositional language we uncover the truth. When you call out a bullshit belief and learn to laugh at it, it loses power.

So if you're thinking 'What if . . .?' – like I was when I met my linen shirt man – do yourself a favour and answer your own question. If you don't you will just keep hold of the uneasy energy, and it will prevent you from sustaining your manifestations.

Here's how to make yourself irrational, for your own good.

Exercise: The What If–What If Showdown

1 Write down a true affirmation related to your vision: mine was, 'I am so happy to be with the love of my life, he is exactly perfect for me.'
2 Now write down all your negative what ifs (What if he dies? What if he leaves me? What if he cheats?).
3 Write down the answers to your own questions (So what if he does die? Then what? What will you practically do? Can you handle it, or will you die too?). Go to the very worst-case scenario, face it – and ask yourself what would you do if that were to *actually* happen?
4 Take your list of questions and answers and tap through the points on each one, one at a time, saying the what if and the answer out loud.
5 Next, dissolve the power of this belief by making up outcomes that are as ridiculous and as negative as possible. Go on – make it really preposterous! Add stats to debunk the belief (for example: What if he leaves me? I will *never* ever find anyone else again in this universe of a billion single men. I will be an old spinster and never recover from this, ever. I will lose all my self-respect and never even go out in public again.). Say it and witness what you're saying like you're observing it through the eyes of someone else. See how silly it is as a belief. You are an empowered, wonderful human. You will cope just

as you've always coped. You are OK. Keep calling BS on your belief. Make it as irrational as you can. Tap through this for as long as you need to.

6   Now it's time for the showdown! Once you feel a shift (you might smile, laugh, pull a puzzled face, cry) and the negative belief loses its power, replace your original negative what if with a positive what if (for example: What if he *doesn't* leave me and instead we have a wonderful happy life together and it stays as good as this?). As you do so tap on your collarbones and heart area. If you say this with truth and believe it to be possible, it will instal a better belief into your system and lead you one step closer to manifesting and sustaining your initial affirmation as a reality in your life. You can finish with a soothing head hug, holding one hand over your forehead and the other over the back of your head.

MAKE SURE YOU SPEAK YOUR OWN LANGUAGE

All your experiences have been processed into your body with a mix of senses, or (as we call it in neuro-linguistic programming), different representational systems. As an NLP practitioner, I work with the presupposition that we operate from a series of past patterns, which have been deeply ingrained in our minds. Your 'primary representational system' (VAKOG for short) is based on these senses, and defined by whichever sensory system you tend to lean on most:

- **Visual** – Seeing, creating pictures, remembering spaces and shapes
- **Auditory** – Hearing, creating sounds, remembering a song
- **Kinaesthetic** – Touching, feeling, trying it, feeling it
- **Olfactory** – Smelling
- **Gustatory** – Tasting

When I'm working with a client I quietly watch out for this so I can help them access their various hidden aspects quicker, and also to bring me into rapid rapport with their unconscious mind. If you think about it, when you meet someone you tend to be drawn to them or not. It's often totally energetic: a frequency match. Sometimes it's a trauma-bonding experience – the sensing of each other's wounds – but often it's down to how well your minds match the information you're giving and receiving. When your new pal says, 'I see what you mean, I see how big your job must be for you,' then they're a visual experiencer. If your boss keeps saying that it 'sounds like it's a big idea' or 'hears this could be difficult', chances are that the boss is an auditory experiencer. I am a very visual kinaesthetic and so I really do need to 'feel' something, and I see strong depictions in my meditations.

Knowing more about the way you process everyday information will help you unlock faster on an unconscious level. When it comes to manifesting with Rapid Tapping it acts like a shortcut to a successful outcome by communicating with your own subconscious. It's like speaking the same language with your memories, rather than trying to speak patchy French and ordering *fruits de mer* and expecting a bowl of fruit to arrive (vegetarians beware – it's a massive plate of seafood). There are lots of good, free online tests you can take around discovering your primary representational system, so have a go at that.

We tend to lean towards a particular 'rep system' so when it comes to our tapping sometimes we access an emotion from a memory when we least expect it and it all surfaces again. Like when you hear an old song, taste a food or smell a perfume and are instantly transported to the emotion behind the memory. Your brain is repeating it all again, and, remember: it doesn't know the difference between what is real and what is imagined.

Reminding yourself of a bad memory, however unconscious it may be, instantly impacts your frequency. In EFT these multiple layers of how we attach ourselves to a memory are known as 'aspects' – different parts of an experience, different layers of how we process information in the nanoseconds that make up a memory. If you had a car crash no doubt you remember certain things, like the way it felt in your body, or the colour of the other car that hit you, or the weather. But you may not have consciously remembered the bearded face of the man who was driving the car, and yet you have this weird feeling about beards that you can't put your finger on. Or the smell of a tuna sandwich ... because someone was eating one in the back seat at the time of the crash. Going into the altered state of tapping, hypnotherapy and other treatments can help access these many aspects that are often latent, hidden from us. So when we tap we can often hit upon these and reduce the emotional charge behind them.

Of course, aspects of memories may pop up years after the event; the overall energy of the experience you think you have cleared might also come back when you least expect it, interfering with your manifesting. I remember when I thought I'd cleared out all my old guff from my ex-husband and that painful divorce. I thought, yep, I'm over it and I can truly look at him with compassion now. I was in a good place. I did all the work, the clearings, the taps, but then I noticed a problem: the old pain was still affecting me. It was as if all the men I could potentially love with my whole heart could also let me down. My energy was not yet in a frequency of total trust and surrender; I was trying to control my relationships by keeping one foot out of the door, one leg out the duvet. However, instead of thinking it might be a failure on my part that I hadn't eradicated the pain and I still had 'work to do', I chose (and continue to choose) to see problems as an invitation.

PAIN IS YOUR PORTAL FOR PLEASURE: PMT (PRE-MANIFESTATION TENSION)

Just before I met my true love, a major invitation to tap into trust unfolded for me. I noticed the synchronicities and they were tense. Exes contacted me out of the blue, people I had loved and trusted started being really aggressive towards me, best friends started being quite tricky, I got a stomach bug – all at once. This is what, in my own understanding, I have come to know as PMT. It's like a really annoying premenstrual tension (PMT), so I call it pre-manifestation tension (PMT). I noticed the PMT presenting itself and went with it. It was time to direct my energy into rebalancing my frequency around love, so I used the techniques in Part One and did a mega clear again! It wasn't as painful as it had been in the past because I realised it was a healing portal for more possibilities to magnetise to me. By reframing the old, dark wounds as opportunities for light to enter, it set me free. Multidimensional manifestations brought me to the place I am at now, blessed to be with my linen shirt man – just like I decided on my vision board that I'd completed only a few weeks before our chance encounter. In Part Two we will learn that manifesting is simply moving from moment to moment. If somewhere along the line the energy drops and we stop acknowledging the positive expression of the day-to-day, we will be in danger of slipping out of vibration with each other. The messy humanness could take over and we might mess it up. But that's not the end of the world, because it will have evolved us.

Manifesting is about diligence to simple kindness and love to oneself and another. If the relationship drops and it isn't in alignment, I am not prepared to stay with someone or something just because I manifested it. That's not the aim with life transformation: there isn't really an 'end' either, just an evolved vision. Trying to keep something 'the same' isn't something the Twelve Universal Laws recommend (we'll learn about these in Chapter 7). They all agree on the eternity of now, the waxing and the waning of all, the chapters and the verses.

You see, our work is never 'done'. I always find new ways to heal and progress – life will continue to yield expansion.

Here's the kinky bit. Pain is your portal for a more pleasurable life and if you use tapping on it (rather than burying it), the energy dissipates and it doesn't last. Try tapping with me now as you affirm this important presupposition once, with feeling.

Tapping exercise: The Pain to Pleasure Tap

SAY IT **Pain is my portal for pleasure.**
Say this affirmation out loud.

After you say it, just sit quietly continuing to tap for a
minute on your collarbones and heart area. Notice where in
your body you feel a connection. Notice the emotions that
come up, or the lack thereof. Just be curious as you tap on
your collarbone points with me.

And again.

Pain is my portal for pleasure.

How was that?

At this point, I don't want you to do a full-on tap routine. Just
say it and notice what happens and keep tapping. We are supposed
to experience pleasure *and* pain because it's like a 'main vein'
way to access our next level. It speeds it all up, gets right into the
motherlode at warp speed. It's a gift. But only if we make a decision
to perceive pain in this way.

If you feel in the mood and prepared to transform old pain into
pleasurable possibility now, take out your journal and write a list
of the five most painful things in your life so far. Remember this
may be a confronting exercise so only start it if you are fully ready.
You can also use finger tapping to sooth any feelings of anxiety as
soon as you finish journalling.

Now, look at each one: you've made a decision to hold onto the
pain. I know that might feel confronting. There's usually a pay-off
for each decision we've made – either consciously or unconsciously.
It might make you feel better somehow to hold onto it – or does it
allow you to keep self-loathing, or maybe to blame someone that
you would be better off forgiving? We don't need to hold onto the

pain any more. We can use tapping to transform it into possibility and get back into pleasure again.

We feel each pain again, shift the energy around it, and move on with our lives. The biggest illusion I see with my clients is that we should wear our pain like a badge of honour and parade it round for everyone else to see. All of us, in pain together. Yippee!

No thanks. That doesn't shine a light of hope on anyone. It keeps us in darkness. This is not what we came here for.

As we know, lightworker Deepak Chopra advocates the idea that our bodies are not designed to hold onto pain, and that our mind–body is one cohesive unit (if we let it be). Our bodies try to help us by reacting to perceived physical and emotional pain. And yet, if we don't tune in to potential next levels and wild goals by using affirmative techniques or tapping away old friction, we risk signing up to a future stuck in the pain. You deserve to lean into possibility and pleasure, over and over again; even if it screws up multiple times, you still deserve to try again.

Get comfy. We are going to tap deeper into debunking this feeling of collective pain-bearing together. I see it come up again and again and it sneakily stops us from accessing new opportunities and growth. It's that feeling, deep down, that we are not *entitled* to experience pleasure, that we are safer if we are in familiar feelings of pain, and that we must stay stuck in painful patterns – just to fit in.

Tapping exercise: The Bring Me Pleasure Tap

Begin with sore spots massage and then tap through the Rapid Tapping points:

SAY IT **Pain is my portal for pleasure.**
Say this affirmation out loud.

SCORE IT How true and believable is this for you as a percentage?

CLEAR IT

- I release any old need to stay stuck in my pain
- My patterns of pain
- They feel familiar
- I see other people in pain
- Therefore I feel like I should too, somehow
- But I am not built for pain
- I was born from pleasure
- I accept and love myself in pain and in pleasure
- I now accept the possibility that pleasure is not wrong
- Although maybe it has felt wrong in the past
- Pleasure is probably something I need to earn
- Pleasure feels a bit over the top
- Surely?
- Or maybe it isn't
- Maybe I can experience pleasure in life
- Possibly
- But at the same time, if I experience pleasure

- That feels like it makes me a bad person on some level
- How dare I have a good, happy life
- When others might be in pain.

CREATE IT

- But on some level, I know that it just makes me a person
- A human
- Who chooses to feel good
- If I feel good, others can feel good too
- Because they see that it is healthy and OK to feel good
- If I choose pleasure, maybe others can be free from their pain too?
- Because they can see it is possible to feel good?
- It IS possible to feel good
- I am so grateful for feeling pain because it's helped me
- My pain has been my strength
- It's a portal for pleasure
- It's a portal for possibilities
- So I courageously choose
- To release my emotional blocks around pain and pleasure
- I'm just a human being
- And I get to choose.

SEAL IT

- I choose pleasure over pain
- I choose possibility
- This is my intention.

SCORE IT Check in again with how believable the original affirmation feels now.

AFFIRM IT
Pain is my portal for pleasure.

> # WARNING
>
> This clearing stuff really works. And the creations that happen once you've made space for new possibilities will attract exciting results. I've seen some of my private clients lose their mind here (because the results can be *fast*) and then totally abandon the continued tapping work. It's like when you're at your first drunken teenage party and you do eight shots instead of one, because you don't have the patience to feel it taking effect. Slow down there, baby! You have all the time in the infinite world.

If you start seeing shifts and changes (you will) you might notice something inside you screaming, 'That's it – I'm sorted!'. If you're manifesting like a machine, you're on a roll and think, 'I'm untouchable! I'm fine now! I'm good to go!', stop! Remember that if you feel pain again (and you will, because you are a human being), or something happens in the world that creates a collective level of high stress (it will), then this feeling is your friend. It is your fabulous portal to access more pleasure, so that even more possibilities unfold in your life.

So if you get sad, anxious flashbacks, feel self-defeating stop signs, sense your inner gremlins coming back stronger ... don't worry – it's because you're being given the beautiful gift of pain as a portal to create *even more*, which may lead to something even better.

Let go. Feel the pain as it comes back, be real and get vulnerable with me. Over and over again.

TAPPING OUT THE BODY PAIN

Often we hold pain and a lack of ease in the body. You could call this dis-ease, even. Tapping is useful for all manner of pain, including that within our body. Nick Ortner, who has championed tapping on a global level, began his love affair with the practice because it eliminated his own body pain. So I'd like to share this next routine with you, which you can use on repeat for minor aches and pains, and for chronic pain too. You can talk to your own doctor about your problems, of course; but as we already know, tapping is effective at shutting down stress. Stress is widely known as the root cause of much disease, so it makes logical sense that tapping effects positive change in this way too.

Working with pain is really to notice that your pain can move, dissipate, change, and that's just unblocking energy. There is something called 'chasing the pain' within EFT, which is relevant here.

What's chasing the pain?

It's about noticing how pain moves and changes. For example, in the following tap routine we're going to focus on body aches, because most of us will experience these at some point in our lives. You can adapt this for whatever you're personally experiencing.

And we'll ask questions about where the pain may have come from, emotionally as well as physically.

We know that our subconscious is a very clever little thing. And often, it's just trying to be like, 'No, don't go there. Don't change, stay here' when we know, really, that we *do* want to go there, because the subconscious is where the power lies. And if that's got misinformation, we want to go in there to rewrite our energetic coding. And then we want to imprint something that feels really helpful and gorgeous for us. And that obviously doesn't preclude our body because we have a mind–body that is impossible to disconnect.

For the next tap, which is a deep shift around the body and self-healing, I'm going to invite you to connect with your higher self. This is a way of tuning in to the very superconscious or intuitive part of you that is almost like your soul essence. I think of it as a wise 'all-seeing' me, that exists in all timelines and has already experienced my own future. It's a way to take yourself out of your 'now' body (especially if it's painful for you) and connect into your spiritual entity, which is sublimely freeing. I saw my dad do this many times through meditation, prayer, and you can too with this next routine.

Tapping exercise: The Body Pain Tap

This is designed as a guided tap so it might be useful to enlist the help of a family member or friend to read it aloud as you tap.

Cast your mind back to the Frequency Scale I talked about in Chapter 5. Think about where you're at. What's the feeling there? What's the emotion you can identify with this body feeling? Notice the score from −10 to +10 on the scale, and say it out loud.

BREATHE Begin with just getting comfortable in your space. Take a deep breath in through your nose, hold it, breathe in a bit more air, hold it, and then exhale out through your mouth slowly. Repeat the same steps, this time placing your hands over your heart.

CONNECT And we're going to bring attention to the soles of our feet. Noticing where your feet may touch a surface, allow yourself to sink down and see roots in your mind's eye, going down into the earth to keep you supported. And at the same time feel and scan your body up from your feet, all the way up, through the very bones of you and the cells of your being up, up, up to where your hands are now. And then feel a beam of light moving up around your head and coming to the top of your head, almost all the way through the ceiling – or if you're outside, let it shoot up into the sky. Feel yourself supported from the very bottom of the earth up to the top of the galaxies. And just in the space now close your eyes and be present.

SORE SPOTS MASSAGE We're going to move our hands to the sore spots. Begin massaging with me, all the while taking some deep breaths.

SET YOUR FOCUS Draw attention to what you want to work on, the issues that you want to bring today. Perhaps there's something in your body that feels tense or stressed or there's an ailment or something that you want to work on. Bring your focus to that area so that energy can flow there. And let's say what it feels like:

ACKNOWLEDGE IT
So I have this feeling in my body and it feels like ...

Get specific in the way it feels right now – if it feels like a sort of knobbly neck I want you to say that; if it feels like a dull ache just say that:

- So I notice this feeling and it feels like ...
- And I choose to love and accept my higher self anyway.

Good.

- I have this feeling in my body and it feels like ...
- I choose to love and connect to all the parts of me anyway
- I have this feeling in my body right now because ...
- But I choose to accept that this feeling is here.

Tap through the Rapid Tapping points, one for each statement below:

- All this feeling I am experiencing in my body ...
- I can absolutely feel it right now
- It makes me feel
- It really makes me feel ...
- And I don't want to feel like that, because ...
- I really don't want this pain and tension
- But I feel it

- And I don't want to
- And it makes me feel like something's wrong with me
- Maybe something's wrong with my body, like this isn't just temporary
- Maybe I feel like it's my fault. And that feels ...

DIRECT THE ENERGY TO YOUR BODY And we are going to take a deep breath in through our nose here, hold it, breathe in again and then exhale as a releasing sigh. Imagine you are becoming more in touch with the empty space around you as you do. And just draw attention now to any part of your body that feels like it needs the attention right now. Rub your hands together, wiggle your toes. Intuitively allow yourself not to overthink it and just go there right now. And then let's say: *Even though I have this feeling, it is possible for me to love my highest self anyway.*

Tap on the collarbones and heart area: *This temporary feeling I have in my body ...*

And just noticing it even more now: *All this feeling, at the moment, it feels like ...*

Now take this time to describe how you're feeling as you continue breathing and tapping. If you had to describe how you feel to another person, how would you sum it up? Say it out loud by filling in the blanks below.

Feels like ...
Feels like ...
And it really makes me feel ...

- And I don't want to feel like this
- So I choose to release some of this trapped emotional pain
- It is safe for my body to relax again now.

COME BACK TO THE PRESENT When you're ready, just come back to the place you're in now and reconnect with your feet on the surface. Wiggle your toes, ever so slowly tap on your collarbones and take a few breaths.

Draw your attention to yourself right here, right now in this moment and notice your body again. Very gently open your eyes and continue to tap on the collarbones and heart area. Very slowly open up your hands to receive, take your breath in, and out. Relax your body and give yourself a bit of a stretch and a break.

EMBODY IT At this point you may want to sip some water, move your body around, smile or shake your hands to embody the new feeling. And when you're looking and feeling into that pain, try to notice if it's as intense as it was before – or perhaps it's moved?

And then when you're ready, we're going to do another round of tapping.

CLEAR IT Tapping through the Rapid Tapping points:

- I give myself permission to release myself from any tension and pain and even though I can't get rid of all pain, I believe I could get rid of some

- I accept that this could be possible for me
- I am also releasing their grip on me
- I'm choosing to feel safe in my body
- I'm choosing to feel safe within my mind
- And I'm choosing to feel safe in my spirit
- And all these tensions I'm holding my body I'm very grateful for because it's my body doing its job
- But I could release some of it now, releasing some of the tension.

Closing your eyes and holding your heart space, ask yourself intuitively – what do I need to release right now? Allow yourself to acknowledge and release any emotion that is associated with your body right now. Let it go; you don't need it any more.

CREATE IT Tapping on your collarbones and heart area, allow yourself to notice the shift you've created within yourself:

- I release myself
- It feels good to release
- And I choose to love and accept my body completely
- I choose to love and accept myself completely
- I choose to love all parts of me
- I choose to accept the now
- I choose to accept myself now, even if I have some remaining pain
- I am enough
- Just as I am.

BREATHE, SMILE AND RECALIBRATE Smile as we tap here a little longer. Then tap on the crown of your head and smile. Take a couple of nice breaths, in and out, in and out.

RECEIVE THE CHANGE Now hold your hands up to receive, rotate your shoulders and just come into your body a little bit more. Rub the palms of your hands together, creating heat, and raise your hands up above your head as you do this, until your arms begin to feel it! We're going to finish off with a head hug. So place one palm on your forehead, and the other on the back of your head, and just hold. Just take this moment to celebrate yourself for shifting energy, creating space and realigning.

EMBODY IT Beautiful work! Now shake it off, take a stretch and come into your body again. You may feel that when you think about your body, right now, there may be a stronger sense of compassion. And the wheels that are turning for you could feel really hopeful and happy. And if that is the case, we can finish this tap by sealing in that connection. If you don't feel a shift, continue to repeat the tapping part of this routine. If you do feel a shift into positive frequency, or a change in your body, use the following tap to seal it in:

SEAL IT So tap with me and notice any good feelings that you have towards your body. And say that feeling out now:

I now feel . . .
I now feel . . .
I feel . . .

Breathe in through your nose and exhale through your mouth.

Repeat.

Beautiful. Well done.

Remember that this can be quite a deep process, and that sometimes it doesn't quite connect the first time – it just depends on you. So be gentle. Repeat this tap when you experience body pain. Take different sections of the body and start to work with them. There is strength in your vulnerability.

As Brené Brown said in her seminal TED talk:

> *'Vulnerability is not weakness; it's our greatest measure of courage.'*

So, if you have agreed that you'll keep courageously clearing out the past that no longer serves your future, then you're ready for Part Two. What comes next then?

Well, the fun part. We're going to start with truly honing down and expanding your vision. Who are you? What do you want? And where do you want to be? Get your journal out – and join me in a few exercises designed to unleash your imagination, dreams and desires.

PART TWO

Create

So what *does* come next? This is an intoxicating question: if you could do anything (you can) and your options were limitless (they are), what would you choose to do? I'd love you to go back to your vision manifesto. Could you make it even more powerful? Even more exciting?

It's now up to you. It's about focus. Shift your energy away from all that isn't working for you and put the power behind the results you actually want. Putting your focus on your intricately honed vision is the next step.

How are you feeling, having worked your way through Part One? Different? You may well feel exhausted – you could be feeling a little overwhelmed. Or you might have a burning fire raging through your belly and can't wait to get creating.

As is the case with most of my clients at this point, you'll probably be feeling calmer and more curious than usual because you're discovering what it feels like to operate in a less negative frequency. Your nervous system is thinking, 'Oh, hang on . . . Don't you need all this stress, though? Have some more cortisol, have some more alert signals!' And you're like, actually, maybe I'm OK? I know how to deal with it now. I can tap on that, thank you very much.

You'll also be in a state of nervous excitement: that feeling that there might just be something *more* for you in store, after all. You can now channel that beautiful energy into the right choices, intentions and behaviours. You can take inspired action, change your habits and start noticing subtle shifts happening all around you.

Have you started to notice synchronicities yet? If not, expect them, because this is where we begin to co-communicate with the universal, quantum energy available to us. Noticing the same numbers, people who you've been thinking about getting in touch, parking spaces becoming easier to find and ideas coming to life. These are all part of what it means to slip into flow.

You're tasting what it will feel like to enter a new emotional state, a different frequency and a positive mindset of pure possibility. Your potential paths do not have to be laboriously paved out; they're already laid out for you. Your frequency might be starting to match the frequency of your vision. Your emotional state is not permanent – there's a new level of freedom coming, because you know deep down that change is the only constant we have.

But entering a new emotional state can often mean starting from zero. Once you clear away lots of old patterns, it can be confusing and exciting as you get ready to enter a new paradigm. It might feel wobbly – that's OK. Imagine you're an astronaut and it's the first time you've gone up into space: you're in a space suit, floating and eating freeze-dried food. Wild. But just because your surroundings are new and unfamiliar, does that mean your whole identity has changed? No – you're just in space and subject to a different set of standards.

You'll find that some stuff isn't feeling as heavy as it used to. Some off days or energy-sucking people are not bothering you as much as they were. Things you used to experience daily, like anger, stress, gossip or negative-selfing, might not feel 'you' any more. You've realised they are just ways to get some temporary relief. You're entering a new paradigm instead of straddling the old and the new timelines of your life!

I want to prepare you for what's to come with some gentle, loving expectation. Embrace what is, accept where you are (even if you still feel rotten and frustrated), and don't resist anything. Stop putting your energy in all the worry. You might be thinking, 'Have I done enough? Is everyone else feeling like they're in a new paradigm, while I just want pizza and a romcom? No, you're on the right track just as you are. Stay curious and intend to raise your energy up now. It's happening. You're reading this for a reason. I'm writing this for a reason. This shit is real.

7 THE UNIVERSE REALLY DOES HAVE YOUR BACK

In this chapter, I'll guide you through the process of raising your energy into a 'plus positive' state, pinpointing the emotions that rise to the surface. Working from this blank canvas, what are your new hopes and expectations? This is when I say to my clients: 'What possibilities are now opening up for you?' The answers are often completely shocking to them. What do I really, truly want? Oh, I don't know. What could I possibly do to change my circumstances? Where do I start? Can I really do this? Hell yes! Like bestselling author and manifesting expert Gabrielle Bernstein says, 'The Universe Has Your Back!' So let's trust it.

CREATING QUANTUM LEAPS

To get creating rapidly, you'll want to tap into your quantum frequency – and to get into that you'll need to learn some very exciting science.

'Why do I need to know about quantum physics, Poppy?'

Well, you don't need to know much, but you do need a basic understanding of the ruling physics behind the workings of the universe. Much of the conversation around manifesting, certainly of recent years, has been at best spiritual poppycock and at worst a toxic cocktail of false hopes. In order to create truly sustainable results – and supported by our understanding of how our brain works – we need to know about the secrets of the entire cosmos. No biggie then, eh?

Don't worry. As you may have guessed, it's all about energy. As one of the world's greatest but little-known minds for pioneering technologies, Nikola Tesla, said:

'If you want to find the secrets of the universe, think in terms of energy, frequency and vibration.'

You're going to need to sit down for the next bit. If you've seen *The Matrix*, you'll remember the scene where Neo reminds himself, 'There is no spoon.' Neo tries not to see the spoon for the metal solid that it appears to be. What he really should be saying is that nothing is fixed in form because we live in a world governed by quantum possibilities, existing as waves of probability and only becoming solid matter when we observe them. The point is that Neo's metal spoon is actually, according to the as-yet-undisputed science of today, 99.99999 per cent energy. And energy is empty space. There's nothing but tiny little atoms moving around there. The same goes for this book, the clothes you're wearing and any-thing you can see.

The thing about the seemingly wacky (yet totally not wacky) world of quantum physics is that it suggests how much power we actually have over what we see and have in our reality.

If multiple paradigms and possibilities exist (they do) and we're not looking at anything but empty space (we're not), then this opens up a Pandora's box of possibility. 'Why don't I already know this, Poppy?' you may be thinking. Well, our largely Victorian education system wasn't privy to this information. Our syllabuses stuck to Newtonian physics, the solid but very orderly way of seeing the world and everything in it. Our complex and unwieldy minds, in my opinion, feel much better represented by a sort of hidden realm of energetic waves running through the universe, waiting to be tuned in to so we can turn them into matter. What a cool, multilayered way to make sense of the world. Even though much more is to be unearthed to fully understand this field, what I *can* lean into is the idea that we have far more control over our lives than previously thought.

Quantum, like any science, is theory so we need to await more proof. It's building predictions all the time, which are consistent with rigorous experiments. And so far, according to Michael Rutherford, author of *Quantum Physics for Beginners*, there have been absolutely 'no failures when using it since it began [in the 1920s] so we would be foolish not to take advantage of it'. And take advantage we have – in terms of inventions, anyway. Telecommunication, solar energy, medical technologies and an entire fleet of new devices have been made possible with this new information. So what about us humans? How do we fit in? What does it mean for manifesting what we want?

Well, we know we are energy too. All is all. Energy is energy. It cannot be made, it cannot die, it can only change form. It is empty space until it is perceived and observed. But it's still there, somewhere in the infinite cosmos that we can't see – but could we feel our way into it?

Perhaps physical matter around us and spiritual energy are

actually the same thing, but spiritual energy is vibrating at a much higher level, which can't be perceived by our five senses. This gives some explanation to the idea of the sixth sense. When you start navigating life with an open mind, leading from the heart, you start to tap into previously inaccessible higher frequencies and access a new world. So, if it all exists on a quantum level *already*, remember; we're *already* abundant – we just need to level-shift (to use a term from engineering) into an increased bandwidth within an infinite spectrum of possibility. We need to modulate our lives to be in vibrational resonance with what we want.

For some, this idea of a sixth sense is nonsense, but for those in touch with their psychic side and intuition, it's very, very real. With practice and faith in the outcome, it becomes a stronger force. It's really up to you to ask yourself: is my current plan working as wildly and fantastically as it could be? And if you have even a whiff of doubt, and you don't like some of the reality around you in an area of your life, then perhaps actively using this quantum technology as your compass– instead of doing the same old thing in the same old way in the same old mindset – might just work wonders for you. Go on – I dare you.

No doubt it's a headfuck, though. But it is possible to let go of the old paradigm and allow this to click for you. So, if you're anything like I was, and you can't get your head around this quantum lark yet . . . fear not. I have a tap for that! It's about allowing uncertainty to exist, and surrendering to your inner control freak that wants to make logical sense of everything. I'm applying this next tap to the concept of quantum physics right now, but if you need to just let go of knowing or controlling everything, in any aspect of your life, then this is a tap for you.

Tapping exercise: The 'Let It Go' Tap

SCORE IT Begin by checking where you are on the frequency scale from −10 to +10

SORE SPOTS MASSAGE

- When I think about letting go it makes me feel ... (*say your intuitive answer quickly here*)
- Because ...
- But I have decided that it is possible to let it go now.

CLEAR IT Tap through the Rapid Tapping points saying the following statements:

- This old way of understanding life
- It's hard to let it go
- It feels familiar
- It's not easy for me to let go of what I know
- It's not easy
- But I accept that now
- It feels uncertain
- It feels different
- But that's OK
- Because it is possible for me to be calmer about not knowing it all
- I am able to choose a more loving frequency.

CHECK IT Pay attention to your body, as you check whether your score on the frequency scale changed.

CREATE IT Tap through the Rapid Tapping points as you repeat the following statements:

- I am willing to choose a new way
- I am able to let go and see what happens
- It will feel unfamiliar
- But I accept and love myself
- I'm ready for this
- So it's perfectly OK to feel this way
- I am trusting that there is something more for me
- I am going to try to surrender to something bigger than me
- That will feel more freeing
- So I am ready for this!
- I let go
- I let it all go
- I step into new possibilities
- With excitement.

Now shake it out, move your body and smile.

CHECK IT Where are you on the frequency scale now?

AFFIRM IT
Right now I am feeling ... about my possibilities!

Give voice to the positive feelings or body responses bursting to be set free!

HACK: Quantum possibilities exist for us – I really want you to get this. Understanding that the universe is operating on a huge invisible platform of energy, frequency and vibration, and that we are too, is the most useful reframe you will ever have in terms of your capacity for success.

CLOCK TIME

Tapping into energetics in terms of your perspective and moving away from a conditioned flesh-and-blood existence, where the ego is in charge and pessimism is hallowed, is the speediest way to quantum leap into your vision. It frees you up from the shackles of 'clock time'. After all, according to scientists much brainier than me, we only have clock time for convenience's sake. It exists simply to organise our days around the rising of the sun, but according to quantum theory, parallel realities exist outside of this dimension and have no interest as to whether you think something will happen either now or in five years. We simply perceive life through a lens ruled by clock time.

We're brought up to be paranoid about running out of time. How many times have you heard yourself, your friends and others say, 'There's not enough time.' If we buy into this idea we are condemning ourselves to a life that's in direct opposition to the concept of quantum manifestation. As I sit here, I've cleared my previous concept of clock time and now see it only as a useful device to schedule my day, but I no longer create my goals with it in mind. In my manifesting process, 'Pivot into Power', we begin by adding a timely element to what we want, just as a target – but then we remove it and let quantum in instead so as not to limit ourselves to traditional societal concepts of how long things 'should' take on life's clock.

When you start to tap away your previous beliefs around something being clock-time-dependent or 'proper' compared to people, you really start not to give a toss about other people's judgement of how soon is too soon, and you open up to infinite possibilities. Your focus isn't then on 'what happens if it goes wrong or fails', and instead you can just get on with having fun in life. Think of it this way: you're simply tuning in to a parallel reality that is *already* out there for you. You've just done the work unlearning what is and isn't possible, and quantum physics tells us we're not subject to the rules we thought we were. Woohoo!

So, what if you decided to tap into these secret possibilities? What if you swapped all that time-related 'can't do it' energy for an aligned groove within a higher frequency?

Exercise: WTF is time?

1 Write down three time-based beliefs you have about achieving a desire. What you want, and how long it will take to manifest it. Think about some wild massive goals (like setting up a business or marrying or retiring) and some small desires (like reading a book, or making dinner).

2 Think about how you're ruling things out because you've been led to believe how long something should take, for example an executive-level promotion, when to have your first child, making the leap to homeowner. All these things are shackled to a set of time-related beliefs

(and *most* of them revolve around getting resourced by money, which we will tap into later).

3   Rearrange what you have with new timelines just for fun – make some really long and some really short. Debunking this time-based belief system is liberating, because you're then able to tap into more magic and less impossibility.

Excuses about time are often linked to our inner control freak, or a deeper belief.

For example, my client is a smart-as-you-can-get woman who has a big hang-up around 'finding a husband'. She thinks it will take about five years and she wants children so she's in a very funky frequency about it all. Let's call her Sarah. Notice how trying to control a step-by-step 'life plan' according to clock time adds to the frequency of tension and panic? This is because if one thing doesn't happen within the set timeframe, everything else seems less likely to happen. I've called out the fears giving weight to the belief too, so you can see what's fuelling the energy behind it. Ask yourself – knowing what you now know about manifesting positively from a place of possibility – do these time-based beliefs curtail her?

CASE STUDY: SARAH'S BELIEFS

1   I should go out with someone for at least one year before I move in with them. (*Because maybe it will go wrong or my partner might think I'm moving too fast.*)

> 2   I should move in with someone for at least a year before we marry. (*Because I need to test out what it will be like in case it fails. He will need at least this amount of time to make a decision about whether he wants to marry me. I have to get married or my mum will judge me and my friends will think I'm 'different'.*)
>
> 3   I want a baby, but it will take approximately two years to get pregnant once I'm married. (*But what if I need IVF, because then it will take me even longer? I'll freeze my eggs now just in case and give myself an extra year.*)

The entire energy of this outcome is all about controlling the situation based on fear gremlins. The beliefs are not fact, but are sneakily fuelled by comparison and social culture. I had another client who was single for nine years and within weeks of working with me she had met her future husband by chance and was meeting his parents and moving in with him. I believe this was because I helped her change her mindset over how long something was meant to take and reduced the false belief that she would be single 'forever'. Combining this with relevant tapping on the core themes achieved a positive outcome. When we control time based on the limitations of 'clock time', we are trusting our tiny human brain to know all the answers based on the life we have led thus far.

Cue the terror within my client, Sarah: 'Poppy, I really need to date every man on my dating app within the next twelve weeks because if I don't, my whole plan will fail, and I will end up miserable and alone.' This 'plan' felt useful, as it probably ticked all the boxes in coaching frameworks (she had her SMART goals all lined up and an action plan) and she'd done all the personality-matching profiling. But what about the energy of it? The so-called plan simply perpetuated the myth that Sarah was not worthy of living her most abundant life.

HACK: If this resonates with you, tap between the eyebrows now and repeat with me: 'If not this, something better.'

I suggested to Sarah that we tap on the concept of time and control. If she was able to reduce the emotional attachments associated with lack of time, and open up to the beautiful concept of manifesting quantum possibilities, might her chosen result rapidly spring into action in a way she hadn't expected? If she decided to surrender to the idea that there's such a thing as 'divine timing', where the magic happens because we trust in something bigger than our own minds, would the result change? You bet.

Try this tap to help you see the concept of time in another way:

Tapping exercise: The 'I've Got No Time!' Tap

SAY IT AND SCORE IT

I create time with ease in an abundant universe

Say this affirmation out loud.

Take a moment to consider how true it feels for you right now as a percentage.

SORE SPOTS MASSAGE

- I feel like time is running out
- I feel like there's not enough time in the day
- I feel like time is not on my side
- Because ...
- But it is possible for me to notice divine timing too.

CLEAR IT Go through the Rapid Tapping points for each statement below:

- I can't always see how it is possible for me to have what I want
- I don't want to lose control
- I want a plan!
- Time is by the clock
- I think I know all the answers
- But maybe I don't
- Maybe I am worrying too much
- I'm spending my precious energy on stressful worries
- What if I let go of this stress?
- What if there was another way to use my time?
- What if I decided to worry less
- And use time positively.

CREATE IT Continue to tap as you go through the following statements:

- I have decided to shift my energy
- There is a field of information over and above what I know

- There is a quantum field of energy out there where time and space exist in a different way
- I am choosing to tune in to new energy
- Quantum physics is interesting for me to know about
- There is an abundance of time
- I am connected to something greater than myself
- This is supporting me
- I love and accept myself.

The real planning needed is in devoting yourself to the techniques I'm sharing with you, not just the 'how' strategy you have in your head. By relying on a fixed plan of action, with little attention to the power of the universe, Sarah was unknowingly cutting herself off from matching the frequency of her dream husband. All the energy was in the plan, and how people might judge her if she didn't have the life she wanted 'on time'. Worse still, she spent most of her time giving energy to the lack, the scarcity and the panic. This doth not a merry manifestor make. So we worked on surrendering to the idea of not having a husband at all. Of accepting what is, and the very worst-case scenario. Ouch. And once she was OK with that, which took some time, she became calmer and more self-loving, which funnily enough has a habit of opening previously blocked-off possibilities. You can probably guess what happened next.

So attracting something into your life isn't really about blindly thinking positively or even pushing a plan, it's about refusing to put arbitrary restraints on your own potential, and believing in infinite possibilities.

MANIFESTING INFINITE POSSIBILITIES

Cool, isn't it? If you thought that I'd be teaching you the Law of Attraction in this part of the book, think again. It is only a small part of manifestation and doesn't tend to work consistently, or, for some people, at all.

The Law of Attraction is powerful and eye-opening, but it isn't the limit of what is useful in terms of effective manifestation techniques. You have to include layers of psychology, physiology and physics too. How can you upgrade your whole frequency to access this quantum realm of infinite possibilities and tap into your superconscious potential? Take Rhonda Byrne's book *The Secret*, which is based on the belief and showcases the spiritual strategies of some of the most successful people on the planet using it. It tells me – and the thirty-five million other people who bought a copy – that thoughts become things insofar as you can think and envision something positively and bring it into your reality.

That *can* indeed be powerful and work well, but only so far as you must believe it to see it appear in your life – and that's hard. How much do you actually believe you can easily and rapidly have a holiday in the Caribbean when you have an overdrawn current account? How much do you believe you can meet the love of your life when you are still tied down by a deep belief that you are not worthy of a wonderful relationship? How can you attract a super-amazing, early-adopter role in your industry when you're crippled with a fear of speaking in public? All these things can be achieved – but not by pretending you're OK. When we resist negativity, we unknowingly assign it more power.

Unless you clear away the power-sapping energy of the limiting, outdated and negative beliefs that don't resonate with the abundant energy of your intended goals, you're going to be disappointed by the results. Unless you can confidently change your behaviour to support your desired outcome, you're slowing down the process. Unless you take confident, consistent action steps towards your goals alongside your envisioning, you're missing the fullness of your potential.

Interestingly, what I've come to learn in the decade that I've practised tapping is that much of the ancient spiritual wisdom is saying exactly the same thing as new science. As a teenager, I started off with a spiritual curiosity, signing up to different religions and schools of thought, but moved into science over the years too. I don't believe they are mutually exclusive. When you compare the core spiritually based laws with those of new science, there are striking similarities. My guess is that somewhere along the lines, previous generations have been forced to choose between two camps: are you a woo-woo New Ager witch to be burned and drowned, or are you a '(wo)man of science' where society (run mostly by men back then) might just take you seriously? Pick one, goddammit! But no: centuries of gender repression and misinterpretation of subtle, mystical energies and traditions are coming back to life again, don't you think? There seems to be a real Age of Aquarius shift where we're less divided and closed-minded about what we use to guide our life with. Life is not that binary; even light and dark are on the same spectrum.

Are you getting into this as much as me? I absolutely *love* living life this way. Let's keep up the high vibe. Let me tell you about the spiritual laws of the universe.

THE TWELVE UNIVERSAL LAWS

The twelve universal laws are thought to be intrinsic, unchanging laws of our universe that ancient cultures have understood, whereas modern Western civilisations often choose to ignore or mock. This is generally just from a lack of knowledge. So I was told by a mentor of mine to learn as much about other civilisations and cultures as possible. When we don't know enough about something, it makes us feel insecure and unsure, which causes a reaction that leaps straight to criticism and attack. You might have seen this in a particularly annoying person before? Stick it on your trigger list – they're just not informed enough!

The twelve much-revered laws (the idea is they are unshakeable and unbiased) can be linked to Ho'oponopono, an ancient Hawaiian practice of reconciliation and forgiveness. Echoes of these laws are seen in many religious texts as parables or underpinnings. They're also referred to as the universal laws of success because some of the world's most dynamic movers and shakers have taken them onboard. This is the part that I find so fascinating: how are the people who feel successful on their own terms making use of these laws? See if you can spot one of these that's taking all the credit (clue, it's the Law of Attraction – and yep, it's just *one* of them).

1 Law of Divine Oneness

'We are all connected and we are all One.'
RHONDA BYRNE, writer and producer

The mothership of all the laws because we cannot operate as separate individuals, and all the other laws build upon trusting in this one. If we've had a lot of hard knocks, or we do not identify as spiritual or we've been burned by religious doctrines (Catholic guilt anyone? Convent schoolgirl present and correct here) then it's harder to believe we are actually all divinely connected as One. We are born to operate on a superconscious level with innate knowledge, and it is fully possible to tap into this interconnectedness for miraculous results. Work on believing in and activating this one, and the rest will follow.

To go deeper, everything within you is connected to everything outside (or without) you. This means what is within is also what is without. You are literally at one with the very make-up of the universe because every atom inside your body is connected to the rest of everything in the world. This suggests to me that there is a very original creator of sorts – a God, an Energy, a Source. Because I don't see my personal God as a bearded white guy in the sky, I choose to say God, Source, Energy – all as One. When you are tapping you are affecting not just yourself, but the entire collective. When you are helping yourself, you are giving back to the planet because your frequency is rising. Bravo. Tapping is very unselfish self-help.

2 Law of Vibration (or Frequency)

'Nothing rests; everything moves; everything vibrates.'
The Kybalion

Everything in us, and around us, is energy vibrating. We are just human vibrators, am I right? And the batteries can run low sometimes, but if we're plugged into the main socket, we are capable of a very high voltage result! This is saying that everything is on a frequency; particles are constantly on the move and we are always going towards or against something. Tapping is designed to raise your frequency and your vibes so you can attract more of what you want. If you want to *receive* love, you'll want to vibrate in a frequency *emitting* love so you can dial into more love. Trying to get more love when you are a ball of hate is not the same vibe.

3 Law of Correspondence

> *'I alone cannot change the world, but I can cast a stone across the waters to create many ripples.'*
>
> MOTHER TERESA

We are a product of our subconscious beliefs because we repeat ourselves, either helpfully or unhelpfully, in patterns and loops, which ripple out and are felt throughout the universe as a collective energy. We can break these habits within ourselves and replace negatives with positives using tapping. We self-correspond and correspond with others on a loop based on what we feel, and there is a direct link between how we feel on the inside and what we experience on the outside. We can be change-makers for the future in how we show up today.

4 Law of Attraction

'Our thoughts, our feelings, our dreams, our ideas are physical in the universe. That if we dream something, if we picture something, it adds a physical thrust towards the realisation that we can put into the universe.'

WILL SMITH, actor

Like attracts like. The most popular law out there but, again, only one of the twelve. Your mindset and self-worth are like a handy mirror to the reality we live in. All around us is a completed jigsaw puzzle that is an outcome of beliefs, decisions, and actions according to our past, but at any moment we have the power to remove pieces, tap by tap, and create an entirely new picture.

It's hard to attract something when our belief system is off, and this is why I bang on about clearing a lot within the process of creating. You have to *believe* what you want is possible to have. Essentially, this is Law of Vibration in motion: your emotions and what you feel reflect what you attract to you, so you are quite literally tapping into your dreams. However, we are part of a bigger collective of other vibes, so we can't control everything on the exterior plain. Taking as much radical responsibility here for your inner game is what helps set you emotionally free, because a blame culture is a very low frequency. That blocks you from receiving. It's like wearing metal armour into the shower and expecting to be cleansed.

5 Law of Action

'Vision without action is a daydream. Action without vision is a nightmare.'

Japanese proverb

There's action – and there's inspired action. Once you've tapped on your outdated beliefs and old patterns, and you've got a vision to go get, then you can take control of the momentum you've built and change things up. Small, focused actions immediately after a tap are always advised! You're in a good energetic alignment post-tap, so use it or lose it. Take one small action towards your vision after each tap, because it will be from a superconscious place of inspiration and flow rather than daily drudgery.

If you can take one action now, do it – and take time to tap each day. Reading this and then not putting what you've learned into practice is not actually tapping in at all, it's just inaction. Pursue your desires with a can-do attitude, go beyond your comfort zone, do it without fear of success or failure – it is all just experience and stepping stones towards the next manifestation.

6 Law of Perpetual Transmutation of Energy

'The secret of change is to focus all of your energy, not on fighting the old, but on building the new.'

SOCRATES, philosopher

Bit of a mouthful. You can redirect each emotion into a positive if you redirect the energy behind it. Nervous energy can be changed within a tap to become calming energy, which you can use to infuse peace into your working day. Rage can be channelled into passionate sex energy and we can channel bored energy into our creative pursuits or a new habit. Noticing the energy, rather than looking for the reason why, can allow us to step back from the problem to swap the focus. It's not binary – we can enjoy the journey and the nuance towards our greater lofty goal that feels far away, like 'I want to be happy.'

7 Law of Cause and Effect

'A life without cause is a life without effect.'
BARBARELLA, fictional sci-fi character

Also known as karma, it is believed in many schools of religion such as Buddhism, Sikhism, Hinduism and Taoism. This is the idea that every action will also have a reaction – positive or negative. The energy that you bring to the cause of something will have a ripple effect; it will underpin your future actions. For every effect you see, there is a cause somewhere along the line. We think of this as mostly action begetting action, but the way you talk to yourself, and about others, also falls into this. The cause of something is the effect of something else and this relates to your manifesting game. This principle requires us to acknowledge the effects of our thoughts, actions and behaviours because if we do, we can transform them to bring about more positive effects. This law tells us that we don't necessarily see the effects all at once, but they will pop back up. Trust that if you transmute energy from hate to love, then you're more likely to manifest loving results.

How to tap into this:

Tapping exercise: Using a self-karma diary

1　Revisit the concept of a self-talk diary, but this time note down your positive and negative self-talk and see it as a karmic command centre, noticing the after-effects of each command you give yourself.

2　Find any negative causes from your own mindset and see the connection to the actions you took (or didn't take!). What self-karma are you creating? If you don't like some of the results in your diary, thread back and notice the energy you put into the cause of this. Can you make any changes to the vibes you put out there in the future? To change your self-talk karma, go through the Rapid Tapping points as you say aloud each self-administered *cause* behind each effect, releasing the emotional charge.

3　Then maintain an after-effects diary for a week to keep track of how you feel following each tap, and to note down any subsequent new positive actions taken.

8 Law of Compensation

'Each person is compensated in like manner for that which he or she has contributed.'

RALPH WALDO EMERSON

This means we will only get what we give out as energy. Tapping is the way to become a clearer receiver (so many of us are great at giving but terrible at receiving). Just think about accepting compliments – do you happily receive them? Because if you reject them, you're saying sod off to the universe's rewards. Hard as it might initially be, learn to be a taker as *well* as a giver. And if you're too much of a taker, start sowing some seeds of generous intent. Similarly, if you reframe your life to become more positive you will start to notice more positives around you. This so often comes up around money – you work and give, accept the reward! We live in an abundant, unbiased universe.

9 Law of Relativity

'How someone else processes your truth is not your responsibility. Their reaction says much more about them than it does about you and your truth.'

FEARNE COTTON, *Speak Your Truth*

Nothing is actually 'good' or 'bad' – it's just there. It's relative to something out of our control and that's OK. We so often plague ourselves with strong opinions of what is 'right' and 'wrong', but at the end of the day this means *we* are the ones attaching meanings to neutral expressions of life. *We* are the ones applying emotional charges to neutral tasks and experiences. Thankfully, your tapping will help clear the opinions that are not serving you. For example, someone in another part of the world or a different religion, custom or civilisation, couldn't give a toss that you think you're fat. They don't think that way. To them, *you're* wrong. Because you're too thin. This law can be strengthened by perspective and honouring our own authenticity, so where can you find evidence for a new perspective today? Like maybe you *are* good at what you do, you *can* do the thing you're dreaming up and it *isn't* wrong to follow your heart.

10 Law of Polarity

> 'We humans love to compartmentalise things. We love to
> divide our education system into different subjects, just as
> we divide our shared planet into nations and our books into
> separate genres. But the reality is that things are blurred.'
>
> MATT HAIG, *Reasons to Stay Alive*

This idea is that everything in life has a direct opposite – hot and cold, love and hate, good and bad – and that it's all the same thing, on a sliding scale. In the Frequency Finder Scale (Chapter 5), you will see that negative is just the absence of positive, but they're both expressing the same thing on the same scale: emotion. We think everything is wildly different but in fact they're not, they're simply at varying degrees. In my own work, if I want a client to shift energy, I ask what can be done to command the opposite emotion. Doing something that makes you happy when you're feeling sad sounds obvious, but what about doing something to remind yourself just how alive you are when you're feeling dead to the world? Like dancing in your pants. The lower you've been, the higher you can go. Look up instead of down wherever possible. And if you can't – SOS tap!

11 Law of Rhythm

> 'For everything there is a season, A time for every activity
> under heaven. A time to be born and a time to die. A time to
> plant and a time to harvest.'
>
> Ecclesiastes 3:1–8

We are all moving in perpetual cycles and stages of development according to a natural rhythm. We have down days and up days. We have quiet periods and active periods. The trick here is to accept this and not to do ourselves down when we want to rest. We can see life as stages and chapters, new beginnings and endings. Our universe is built this way, and so we must not resist the natural tides of our lives and emotional health, nor push, push, push until we burn out. If you're overdoing it, underplay it with a quiet rebellion. There is an art about doing nothing, yet leaving nothing undone. Seasons – we don't argue with the fact that winter comes – where in your life are you bemoaning (pointlessly) winter? Spring will come. Have faith. Wait. Have a mojito.

12 Law of Gender

'I love a soul, not a gender.'

SOPHIE TURNER, actor

This one is basically less about the body parts, more about the energy. Just speak to someone who doesn't identify as their birth sex; it's about the way they feel, the energy inside, their spirit. Rather than seeing ourselves as a 'woman' or a 'man' in a binary way, we can identify as a whole soul with various expressions. The concept of divine feminine and divine masculine is something I often teach my clients. In modern times, and particularly within my work in the female empowerment space, I have seen a worrying focus on the 'hustle harder' attitude. Slowing down to speed up is about nurturing the quiet, peaceful 'pulling' energy as well as the more active 'achiever' side of ourselves. Have you ever felt 'off' and sought balance in your energy? Of course you have! Working with predominantly high-achieving women has hammered home to me that we're often ignoring one side of ourselves: the yin – quiet, resting goddess energy mostly. Some of my most magnificent manifestations have come from spending days alone tapping, meditating and practising yin yoga in my divine feminine after a very 'yang' (busy, active) time with my career. It's about balancing the gender energies and not being deficient in either. Ancient mythology is snazzy here; they were much more open than we seem to be nowadays about gender, trans and embodying uniqueness.

The gist of all this is that we are, above all, a spirit having a human experience and that is a freeing thought. (Phew).

So, if you're ready to bring these laws into your life, let's get into the business of creating with what we command.

8 SAY IT WITH ME

The massively fun part of the book is here! It's time to maximise your use of affirmations with tapping. You've probably heard of 'positive affirmations', which exploded in popularity on social media in about 2018 – I can't scroll through my Instagram feed these days without spotting a T-shirt slogan saying 'Go Girl, live your dreams. You can do it!' But when it comes to tapping you may not have used *true* affirmations before – and be unaware of the possibility that you might be using *negative* affirmations.

I've been using positive affirmations since I was about seven or eight years old. I had Post-it notes all over my mirror and a jar filled with pieces of paper with different emotions and quotations written on them. Each morning I would practise affirmation work in the mirror (a very powerful exercise to try with tapping). I had more *carpe diems* up on my bedroom wall than I had boy band posters, that's for sure. As a little girl from Cornwall with a big imagination and a clear vision, many of the affirmations I used came true: all the A*s in my GCSEs, an early marriage, a first-class degree and a big media job in London. But I came to know that sustaining what we affirm is a whole other matter, and we'll come back to this idea in greater detail later. For now, let's focus on how we use affirmations alongside our work in energetics to create what we desire in the first place.

WHAT IS AN AFFIRMATION?

I define affirmations 'as a self-induced communication device to your many layers of consciousness so you can raise your self-worth and self-belief to the place where you're resonating at the frequency to manifest'. Think of them as commands. You're telling all the layers of your consciousness that something is the new normal, over and over again.

They're our way of taking back power in our lives. They're positive reminders or statements that can be used to encourage and motivate yourself or others. Often it's a lot easier to affirm others than it is ourselves, but we need to remember to encourage ourselves first. If used correctly, alongside tapping, you can use them to accelerate real results in your life.

Here are some of my favourite general positive affirmations:

- I believe in myself.
- I have the ability to succeed.
- I love and accept myself completely.
- I can accomplish anything I set my mind to.
- It is possible for me to . . . (*fill in the blanks*).
- I am releasing all the negative emotions from my system.
- I am willing to step out of my comfort zone.
- All is well.
- Everything is exactly as it is, and I accept that now.
- I accept myself exactly as I am.

Research shows that using positive affirmations is incredibly helpful when it comes to achieving your goals and establishing self-worth because they lessen the threat of the unknown. A study of affirmations showed that they broaden a person's overall perspective and reduce the effect of the negative. Researchers have suggested that self-affirmations remind individuals of psychosocial resources that extend beyond a specific threat, enabling them to focus on sources of positive self-worth that transcends the threat. This in turn is thought to reduce reactivity to the threat and protect overall psychological well-being.

As I mentioned earlier, when we want to do new things, or something outside our comfort zone, our nervous system often perceives the change as a threat and reacts. Tapping can help to reduce this 'unsafe' feeling so that we are more likely to feel we can do new things – but what about saying affirmations? Can words spoken aloud really do anything to help us accomplish our desires? Yes, they can – so long as you *believe* what you're saying is inherently as true as possible.

I like to differentiate between affirmations that are mostly just robotic words, and the ones we believe in our heart, by calling them *true* affirmations. You'll know you are using the latter when they come from a true place, with a heart connection and a believability factor of over 80 per cent.

HACK: We need to think about why we're saying affirmations – and the answer must be to achieve a goal we've set for ourselves, based on the overarching vision for our most fulfilled life. If you're not connecting them to something wild and bold, or you're unclear, what's the point?

When it comes to setting goals, I am into the theory of positive psychology, which was developed by psychologists Martin Seligman and Mihaly Csikszentmihalyi. Positive psychology does not recommend something just for the outcome – the emphasis is on the transition to reach that goal. It's about the journey, the way something feels when we do it and the awareness of how we are evolving as we do. The chances are that if we enjoy the ride we will be in a state of flow and ease when working towards our goals (as opposed to a state of panic and fear . . . you get the idea), which will increase the likelihood of achieving true and lasting success.

So what's your motivation here – and are you sure you can enjoy the journey to get to the outcome? If you feel your motivating energy behind the affirmation is coming from a place of control, lack or force, then stop. You can start to discern which 'zones' from the Wheel of Possibility are out of balance and may require some attention and deep tapping. Or, Lord, have mercy on yourself and loosen up, have a glass of vino. Consider all the joy you already have.

Research has shown that having some level of self-affirmation contributes to positive mindset and honest self-actualisation, so take some time to reflect on what you have – and what you value in life. Perhaps your family, your ability to have some finances, the roof over your overthinking (but precious) head, the intelligence you've been fortunate enough to nurture, your friendships . . . It's making us more cognitively aware and more understanding of our flaws, too. Who cares if you felt crap and missed a day of tapping? You'll live. Think about all the other taps you've completed and how much progress you've made! Practising honest self-affirmation alongside the art of true positive affirmations wildly escalates the effectiveness of your manifestation trajectory because you are primed for peak performance in your action and reactions.

In fact, while we're at it with the stats, a study of brain activity between those who self-affirmed and those who didn't before taking action within a task revealed that 'Being our *authentic selves* reduces the defensiveness that can hinder performance improvement.'

Studies have shown us that self-affirmation makes you less edgy when getting bad news, more resilient, more self-controlled and more accepting of criticism, bad work days and even negative health issues. Not bad, eh?

So how do you supercharge your truest affirmations in Rapid Tapping, so they positively change your reality? Use the clearing taps on a regular basis and focus on sectioning and balancing out what you feel is wonky on the Wheel of Possibility. You'll then start to notice that you know intuitively when you want to ride a high energy. When your vibration is on the up, focus on the true affirmation and bodily sensations you are creating. You can create a true affirmation with the 'seal-in' process towards the end of every routine, and here's a humdinger of a whole supercharger routine when you need an extra-special boost.

Tapping exercise: The Supercharger Routine

SAY IT Begin with a sore spots massage and then repeat the following

I feel ...
Because ...
And I know it is possible for me to ...

CLEAR IT Repeat using the Rapid Tapping points as many times as you need.

At the point at which you shift the energy, you will start to notice more positive emotions and better feelings within your body – all you have to ask yourself is whether they feel true?

When you experience a true positive feeling you'll always notice a shift in energy – often this can feel momentous and your whole body will light up and change. As this happens, focus on the emotion and how you experience it. It may change each time you tap.

Some days you might feel 'calm' or 'confident' or even 'bliss' – if that happens you want to extract the most apt word or feeling and create an affirmation around it. Don't overthink it – quickly allow yourself to be led by intuition. Why? Because it's coming from absolutely 100 per cent authentic truth after an energy-shifting routine like this. It is not made up or forced or logical – it is no longer just 'words' – you truly feel it, you know it to be true for you And we manifest from what we feel, so check the emotion and get affirming!

Note: This is a very short, rapid affirmation. You're not looking to complicate it or add a goal. You're simply affirming the truth of what you've created within you and asking for more of this to boomerang back to you by affirming it out.

SEAL IT The next step is to embody the feeling in order to supercharge it. Think of it as the tiny voice within you that's being heard for the first time and believe it and go with it. End by repeating your own true affirmation, or you may want to use one of these examples:

I am CALM
I am FOCUSED
I am CONFIDENT
I am IN BLISS

If you're really into this, then the following five-minute daily create routine can be tagged onto the end of it, specifically for your positive affirmations.

Tapping exercise: The Rapid Daily Create Tap

Use this daily tap if you are feeling in a positive vibration and want to seal that in and invite more positive energy. Before you get started, make sure you have done the daily clearing or feel in a plus-positive state on the Frequency Finder Scale (between +1 and +10).

1 Sit or stand upright. Begin breathing in through your nose and out through your mouth, mindfully.
2 Next, increase your capacity for bilateral stimulation by tapping your feet on the floor, starting with the right foot and then the left – like you're marching.

3   Next, find your sore spots, and as you massage
    them, say this:

I feel... (*add your own seal-in – a true, positive feeling*)
Because... (*add your reasoning – what's making you feel
this way? Pull up a wonderful memory, something you are
currently grateful for. Use all your senses: see it, taste it,
hear it, smell it and touch it! Make it as real as you can in
your mind*)
And it is possible for me to... (*state your positive
affirmation here as a possibility*).

4   Next, smile, laugh spontaneously if you can, and tap
    through the Rapid Tapping points at a more rapid pace
    than usual with pure, positive intention that this is *truly*
    possible for you.
5   When you feel your seal-in level is about 80 to 100 per
    cent true, only then upgrade your affirmation to an
    'I am...' statement.
6   Repeat step 4 with more feeling than ever...
    et voilà!

YOUR TRUE AFFIRMATION HIT LIST

Make it rapid Don't make your affirmations long and
OTT; separate them down into focused bite-sized chunks
of new evidence. Focus on the focus. Keep them clear,
concise and chirpy.

Use present tense Manifesting with affirmations requires a sense of working with the magic of a moment – not the past or the future. The Universal Laws tell us that we attract back what we put out, and so if an affirmation involves wanting something – i.e. implying that something's missing – it can't be as effective. You want to start feeling like you have it already, so eradicate ambiguity such as 'hope', 'will be' or 'one day' language from your affirmations. Use 'I have', or 'I am' or 'It is possible for me to …'

Play with it Have fun – make sure you feel good and expansive when you say your affirmation aloud.

Keep it positive This is not a time to clear like we did in Part One. It's about creating with the energy of possibility, so keep everything upbeat. Keep all language positive (remove the 'don'ts', 'cannots' and 'nevers').

Memorise it Know your affirmation off by heart, so you can connect to your heart as well as your head while saying it.

Put it where you can see it Write it down on a Post-it note, create a digital mock-up of it, or add it to your Instagram.

Truth test it Do you believe this is possible for you when you say it? Truth test it by using the Say It and Score It technique and if it's over 80 per cent it's good to go – if any less, adjust it until it feels more believable for you.

Breathe before and after Clear your lungs of stale air and practise some intention breathwork to top and tail your affirmation work. Always notice your posture: is your body aligned?

Tap whilst saying it Add extra oomph by tapping as you seal it in.

Meditate around it Be still, silent and let your affirmation sink in like a Savasana pose at the end of a yoga class. Relax into it – stay with it longer than you think you need to.

ADDING INSPIRED ACTION TO YOUR AFFIRMATIONS

1. Send your affirmation to some friends – then ask them to text your affirmation back whenever they think of you. **Note** A word of warning: don't ask negative, low-frequency people who do nothing to further your personal growth and actively discourage you from fulfilling your heart's desires.

2. Create one solid action step around each affirmation. For example, if your affirmation is, 'I am willing to step out of my comfort zone,' then how can you *actually* start momentum going there? Can you put a date in the diary? Could you action an idea? Words take hold when aligned action is applied.

3.   Affirm each result by keeping an 'affirmation evidence' list. You can write down and collect evidence of each 'nod' you get towards this affirmation being more true and real.

The Rapid Tapping Affirmation Accelerator

If you'd like your affirmations to accelerate in terms of effectiveness and speed of return, but you're feeling a little wobbly about whether it will happen for you still, use this exercise.

1   Say your own affirmation out loud in the present tense, beginning with 'I am ...' (*e.g., I am calm and confident*).
2   Notice how true this feels to you on a scale of 1 to 100 (*100 per cent is fully true and believable as if it's true for you right now*).
3   Identify the negative feeling(s) around it that show up most strongly (e.g., anxiety, frustration and self-doubt).
4   Now massage your sore spots as you say this:

I feel ... (*add your current feelings e.g., 'stressed and anxious*)
Because ... (*add your reasoning, what's making you feel this way*)
But I decide to accept myself anyway.

Next tap through the Rapid Tapping points as you repeat quietly, focusing on accepting the affirmation.

5   Make it a deep decision. Once you've acknowledged
    and accepted the way you feel and cleared some of the
    subconscious negativity around it, adjust your affirmation
    by adding the idea of possibility into it. It's important
    that our conscious affirmations match our subconscious
    beliefs, or we are at risk of just reinforcing negative
    feelings. So choose yourself, or how can you expect
    anyone else to choose you?

Say out loud:
I *decide* to be ... (*add your own affirmation again*)

Now test how possible and believable this feels out of 100 per
cent again. Chances are it's feeling more real for you now, so it's
becoming a true and meaningful manifestation affirmation (rather
than a wish). Repeat this true affirmation daily until it reaches
80–100 per cent in terms of believability, and keep checking if any
new aspects or blocks come up that you could tap on.

WHAT ABOUT NEGATIVE AFFIRMATIONS?

Just as we have negative visioning, we can have negative affirmations. You are constantly self-affirming and commanding – but
on average are you doing so negatively or positively? You can demo-
tivate yourself on a daily basis without even knowing it. Negative
affirmations can be pinpointed with your detective-journal log of
crappy self-talk that we started in Part One – essentially when you
do yourself down and repeat things that are untrue.

You can spot your own negative affirmations by noticing what your beliefs are, and checking on your own gremlins. These are multiplying like zombies when you say or participate in things which carry a low vibration, like gossip, hate-talk, trolling, bullying, blaming, projecting and relationship one-upmanship. Stop all traces of this. It's not just hurting someone else – it's hurting your own frequency. It's drinking your own poison. You're capping your ability to manifest what you want because you're affirming to the universe that you want more of the same bullshit (aka negative horrible situations and feelings).

But what if I feel strongly that something is not just or fair? Do I have to hold it in? Pretend everything is fine? No way – because you now know how to tap, you are safe to let your thoughts and emotions run wild.

If you really want to go the distance with some cause that you feel passionate about, then reduce your sabotaging negative affirmations. Channel that passion for good! I work as an advisor to many organisations (and their leaders) that support victims of horrific human rights abuses and domestic violence such as Women's Aid, the United Nations and Women for Women International. I also have sat on the committee for sustainability for the British Academy of Film and Television Arts (BAFTA), to advise on how to carry messaging of the 'way too late' climate change through broadcast programming. These topics are heartbreaking and difficult to discuss – so I used to ask myself am I affirming this negativity and contributing to a societal frequency of fear? This is a tricky one. I don't have the answers. Many purist Law of Attraction coaches advise that in order to contribute to positive change you can obliterate your discussion of anything negative, stop watching the news entirely – and stay on the sunny side.

The thing is, however, that we need to action change. We can't avoid giving voice to crisis. We can't just keep our heads down and assume anything will change through positive thinking alone. Doing the action, saying the unsayable, even when there's a level of discomfort or fear involved, is necessary for social mobility and global changemaking.

What we could be aware of, though, is the emphasis we place on the soundbites we are reinforcing and the energy they are charged with. We can create affirmations of what is already positively changing and affirm that more. We can switch focus into what could be done well, rather than what has been done badly. I try to state the facts (even if they're gross) and put my charged emotion into the possibility that could come if we do X and Y and Z, making sure I'm providing as much constructive criticism as I can. It's not easy to notice our words and redirect the power of them, but I've realised that if I can pour loving kindness into something even when it's hard, I'm pleased to be effecting change in my own way. I'm part of a ripple effect and so are you. If in doubt, tap, affirm what's working and do one thing that will make a tangible difference.

> **HACK:** We can direct our anger towards a situation into action to create an active result rather than a negative feeling. This in turn fuels potential energy, which opens us up to fresh possibilities that resonate in the same frequency.

WHEN POSITIVE AFFIRMATIONS GO WRONG

Here are the top five fails to watch out for, and what to do about them.

1 It's not what you truly want – it's what you think you *should* want

A values check helps here, so regularly repeat the exercises and journal prompts I've provided so far. I also recommend the work of one of my own mentors, Dr John Demartini. Are you asking for what you *really* want, or is it what your mother/partner/boss/co-worker wants? Much of this can be accessed and clarified by having private one-to-one sessions with a life coach or tapping practitioner. Having a clear and heartfelt set of desires is crucial when it comes to affirming something as a reality. If you're doing it for someone else it won't be as punchy and effective, and the energy it carries will be misaligned.

2 It's in fantasy land

This is when an affirmation is just so pie in the sky that you cannot get behind it in your many layers of multi-consciousness. If your affirmation feels too out of reach, please remember to pull it back. You are much more likely to create what you want if you get more realistic in a specific area and then build up incrementally over time once you see the evidence coming into shape. There is a real difference between dreams (feels exciting and potentially possible) and fantasy (feels impossible and escapist).

3 It's not a burning desire: it's a nice idea/it's full of 'buts ...'

I want you to have a burning fire in your belly behind your affirm-ation, so that it feels expansive and exciting. If it doesn't ring true, we can use tapping to clear the nagging issue beneath it. This is more of an intuitive process (right brain) than a 'work it out' (left brain) process, so you'll need to trust your gut in sensing if it's a believable desire.

In EFT there is a useful process around affirmations called 'tailenders'. These are contradictory beliefs that pop up to sabotage an affirmation or a dream/goal. They are clues to the core issue that you might be able to tap on. It's almost as if, when you say the affirmation, there's a subconscious worry that intuitively rears its head when it senses that your dream might become a reality. What would you lose? What in your life might change? What does it mean if you start living what you're affirming?

If you start hearing the gremlins, the voices and the 'yes, buts ...' as soon as you practise saying or writing an affirmation then there are some possible problems to troubleshoot:

- The affirmation is not your *true* desire, but someone else's. It's a should, not a joy.
- It has a weak 'why' attached to it. Check your needs and values to ensure you have a stronger set of positive reasons behind why you're even saying the affirmation. Why are you affirming it?
- Your belief system isn't quite ready for it. We can change that with tapping into the core clearing issues that come up but also through conscious actions that validate our progress step by step.

Try to spot your own tailenders by using my 'Double But' process for identifying the negative 'buts' behind your affirmation and installing a better 'but' in its place:

Exercise: The 'Double But' Technique

1 Say your affirmation aloud and write it down.
   E.g., I believe in myself. I have the ability to succeed.
2 Write down every negative 'but' that pops up for you. These are your inner gremlins, imps and practical objections. For example:

- But ... I don't believe I can succeed because I haven't got a job right now.
- But ... If I succeed my friends will think I'm showing off.
- But ... My dad didn't believe in me, why should I?
- But ... All my life things have gone wrong for me.

3 Now double-but it! Add an extra positive 'but' that evokes the possibility of change. For example:

- But ... I don't believe I can succeed because I haven't got a job right now – BUT I might get one next month.
- But ... If I succeed my friends will think I'm showing off – BUT it might help them to see that they can also succeed.
- But ... My dad didn't believe in me, why should I? BUT that's just one person in a world of a billion others and it's possible that he was only able to believe in me as much as he believed in himself.

- But ... All my life things have gone wrong for me – BUT today is a new day and something might change for me.

4 When you have the 'double but' list ready to go, tap through the points as you say each one aloud, expressing and releasing any emotion as you go. Et *voila*! Sexy buts all round.

You can practise further healing, if you wish, by doing the following:

- Go back to The Big But technique in Part One to deepen your emotional progress.
- Add any of your own negative affirmations to your trigger list, if they feel like meaty ones. And you can go to the corresponding rapid routines in Part One to reduce the core emotional attachments around them.
- Do something that makes you happy. Manifesting is not about getting stuck in the healing process for ever, so swivel into joy and pivot into power as much as you can.

4 It's mindless, not mindful

If an affirmation is just said or written robotically, or like you're spouting off a shopping list, then it won't work. It is absolutely no use saying something without any degree of feeling. Like when someone kisses you without passion, it's gross – and akin to snogging a dead badger. Nobody wants that.

Make a weak affirmation devoid of feeling and you're asking for a limp result in return. Watch YouTube videos while you're tapping and you're splitting your focus. Here's how you can conjure up passion and mindful feeling around the art of affirming. How many of these can you start using consistently?

Use a mirror See yourself – this is making a connection to yourself. You can change your life. The queen of affirmations, the late great Louise Hay, wrote in *Mirror Work*:

> *'A mirror reflects back to you the feelings you have about yourself. It makes you immediately aware of where you are resisting and where you are open and allowing. The most powerful affirmations are those you say out loud when you are in front of a mirror, looking deeply into your eyes.'*

Do a rapid tap before you say your affirmation This will clear your mind, reduce your stress and create a cleaner connection to your higher self and God Source Energy.

Make it a ritual Look forward to your affirmations by lighting a candle, putting on your favourite music, dancing beforehand or having your favourite things around you.

Say it out loud Notice yourself – is it a wet lettuce or a juicy plum of a statement?

Record yourself This is a good way to communicate with your subconscious, because it recognises and trusts your voice implicitly already. Use your voice memo on your phone or get a Dictaphone.

Visualise around it Feel it more easily by seeing it happen, picture yourself on a stage saying it aloud, notice how you look when you say it – the detail of your face, what you're wearing … Make it real in your mind to make it real in your reality.

Write it down – lots There's research to back this up; and ancient civilisations have used this manifesting technique.

Repeat to reinforce Repeat the steps above across several days – don't just do them once and expect results.

5 It's too comfortable, too vague, too easy

You're not stretching yourself enough. Perhaps you are being a bit generic with your affirmations. Are you worried about failure? There's a difference between playing it safe and being courageous and aligning your affirmations to your overall vision. See if you can raise the game from 'I love myself' or 'I am happy and content' to something more specific, stretchy and exciting like 'I love myself enough to receive a high salary' or 'I am so happy and content to live each day afresh with eight hours of restful sleep.' See if you can add unique desire and passion – you truly want this.

Your affirmations are becoming concise and clear, and at the same time communicating with you and your understanding of the universe. It's now time to take the 'but' work a little deeper via a process that will bring you closer to your envisioned life.

UNSTICKING YOUR CODED STICKERS: THE CREATIVE EXERCISE TO HELP YOU CREATE

If we don't upgrade our energetic coding, our affirmations won't become reality – instead our old coded beliefs will. At this point in your tapping journey you will have brought lots of shadowed subconscious blocks to the surface so let's start by doing something about them. I call this synthesis of energetic blocks our 'coded stickers': let's find out what yours are and how to become unstuck from them.

What are your own coded stickers saying?

Take an hour of your day to brainstorm and blitz this – it's a great technique to change your mindset around what's possible for you to create with affirmations and to reduce your subconscious resistance.

For this exercise you need a mirror, a pen and a big pack of large, blank white stickers on which to write down your own objections. One objection per sticker. Here's how it works:

1. What are you focusing on creating at the moment? Let's take money as an example. You have a goal of getting to a new level of income from your business, or in your career.
2. Now take ten minutes to listen and access your subconscious self with my 'Tapping In' Manifesting Meditation Audio, designed to relax and prime your mind – perfect for this very exercise. (You can download it for free at: www.poppydelbridge.com/ tappingmeditation)

3. Then start creating your stickers as soon as you finish listening. You're essentially creating your unique set of negative beliefs, inner gremlins, all the 'buts ...' and all the objections and naysaying you're becoming aware of in the framework of your subconscious mind and energy field. It's useful also to check back over your notes or discoveries from your work in Part One, which feel more like core limiting beliefs. Whatever you feel could be relevant deserves a sticker – allow yourself to be led by intuition. One intention and coded objection per sticker.

Here are some examples of what you might write on your stickers:

- MONEY: If I have a higher salary, people will think I am not good enough to deserve the money given to me.
- MONEY: If I have a booming business, I will be grey and exhausted and have even less time for myself and my family.
- MONEY: If I am super-rich, I will become corrupt, evil or arrogant.
- MONEY: If I have a higher income, I will be more stressed to keep up with the Joneses, like my parents were.

4. Now get in front of a mirror – preferably a full-length one so you can see all of yourself in it – and place these stickers all over your body. Ideally while you're naked ... and cover your bits with the objections ... then tag me in the photo. Honestly, this courageous step is part of this exercise! We are all vulnerable

humans and coming to terms with who we are but having the power to shift these false beliefs and objections is what gives us all power and strength.

How does it make you feel to see what you are carrying around with you? Emotional? Raw? Silly? Upset? Laughable? You may feel a myriad emotions – let them out as you tap and just watch yourself in the mirror. Remember, you were not born with these stickers on you . . . it's a collection of bad habits, traumatic experiences and learned behaviours that have governed your subconscious and created a very long lie. A story of your life. To do this, we can replace these stickers now with something more beneficial. Remember, our brain is neuroplastic fantastic.

5. As you pull off each sticker, stare at yourself with love, tap with one hand directly on your heart and say aloud with bold power:
    I now release any negative emotion behind my false belief.
    It is possible for me to love myself unconditionally.

You'll notice it's about taking full responsibility for the emotions we have, and also for the meaning we place onto the belief. We do get to choose. We either have beliefs or they have us – and it's time to choose the most empowered response to this and love your whole self for everything, even the shadowy coding. This exercise is like a ritualistic, rebellious act of self-love, while releasing negative emotional attachment with intention and compassion through tapping and mirror work. Putting all your inner beliefs out into the open and unpeeling the repetitive hold they have on you one by one is self-affirming. Unnoticed, these stickers can fester.

6. You could even go one step further and rip up the stickers or scrunch them up and throw them away. You can also burn them safely in a fire. The point is, you're working with the power of intention here as well as your tapping. This is very empowering work that will change your overall results for the better.

This is the first time I've shared this technique, but it's brought particularly supercharged results into my own life. It's a kind of affirmation alchemy.

9 MAKING IT HAPPEN

This chapter is all about creating what you want with the core Rapid Tapping routines, and then learning how to stay in flow once you're in a groove with your tapping. I'll begin by sharing with you the key themes you'll want to tap on when in creating mode, based on the Wheel of Possibility. You'll notice this is mainly about energetic creating but will still encompass energetic clearing. When we are manifesting, we're always keeping an eye on what we can clear.

CORE: UNCONDITIONAL SELF-LOVE

I want to offer up a little more around this core theme of tapping into your relationship with yourself, as you direct your life from within. The centre of this is to continually reinforce true and total self-love.

When I refer to self-love, I mean an unconditional, awe-inspiring and deep soul-level honouring and appreciation of the body, mind and spirit that nobody and nothing can take away from you. Self-love is really the basis of all things.

> **HACK:** If you are harbouring any negative emotion when you think about what it means to love yourself then you are putting a condition upon that love. Tap to make self-love unconditional.

If we cultivate unconditional love – both by giving it out and receiving it – we level-up our frequency and manifest more rapidly. When I am actively manifesting a result, I always turn to my self-love tap, even though I would say this is an area where I'm already at a high percentage, because it's always possible to love yourself more. My years of working on myself and on other people and their emotional blocks have shown me that unconditional self-love isn't just a shortcut to a better life: it's essential.

On the flip side, conditional love is when we need to do something, achieve something or be someone before we are able to receive the love that we deserve, which goes against so many of the universal laws. We might feel that the love we receive is determined by how clever, pretty, polite, brainy and successful we are; the environment we are in, the money we make or the number of social media followers we have. This insecurity is recycled on a loop and it seeps into all aspects of our lives through self-talk. It then affects our relationships, the way we are treated and the way we treat others. You might have seen this play out in your relationships. A client of mine gave me a list of criteria that her boyfriend needed to meet before she would marry him – not that he was aware of it. But don't confuse healthy boundaries with control. Often we refuse to love others – or ourselves – totally, because we are trying to control external factors to reach standards that we believe will make us feel worthy, or to avoid our own perceived imperfections.

It's a vicious cycle, leaving you feeling like you have to do or be something in order to deserve things.

False humility is another stumbling block when it comes to self-love. Within EFT the phrase 'I love and accept myself deeply and completely' is used to set up each tap. But I don't use this because even the most successful, gorgeous and wonderful women I've worked with have a hard time saying this and feeling it 100 per cent. To avoid a conscious conflict, I use the phrase, 'It is possible for me to love myself unconditionally' instead.

We often struggle to say 'I love myself' and mean it, because – certainly in the UK where I grew up – it was assumed that to love oneself is to be egotistical, self-absorbed or arrogant – but that isn't the case. The ego is the vessel in which we are here on this planet. The ego is just a necessary means of us – our soul – dealing with life in this body, but if you strip it away and look at what remains, we've got an infinite soul and that soul is total love. As author Marianne Williamson said in her book *A Return to Love*,

'Our deepest fear is not that we are inadequate. Our deepest fear is that we are powerful beyond measure. It is our light, not our darkness that most frightens us. We ask ourselves, Who am I to be brilliant, gorgeous, talented, fabulous? Actually, who are you not to be?'

Your challenge? See if you can open up to the possibility that we can value ourselves more and more and more – regardless of whether that sounds like we're being too proud, or boasting, or if we've done something we can't forgive ourselves for – can you see what it means to have unconditional love for ourselves? It's extremely powerful – but can also manifest as a terrifying pressure of potential if we are not supported. This is where being in a loving community of other tapped-in people can empower you to progress.

I was blessed to be born into a family who loved me unconditionally. I knew that no matter what I did I would still be loved. As a child, my subconscious sponged that up as an ingrained unquestionable belief. And that propelled me into the work that I do now, because I know so many of us haven't grown up with that stability.

Tap on your collarbones and heart now, and then journal what opportunities would open up if you decided to live according to these three mantras:

I am love no matter what I do
I am love no matter what I say
I am love no matter what I think

This next tapping routine is one of your core tools – repeat it until you are feeling the love for yourself on a true scale. To prepare your logical brain for this tap, write down five reasons why you must, without any internal negotiation, honour and love yourself. Those reasons can be what you contribute to society, your work or something that you need to show someone else, perhaps you're a role model, a parent or a friend; whatever it is, there will be powerful reasons why it is possible and helpful for you to love yourself unconditionally.

If at the moment your capacity for this kind of love is still low, don't worry. I've experienced that too, but now I'm maintaining an overflowing cup of self-love with tapping – clearing any discord and peeling off coded stickers as I go. You too can absolutely step into the unrivalled level and frequency of self-love. Let that possibility happen now.

Tapping exercise: The Self-love Core Deep Tap

We're going to begin by delving deep. This may feel quite intense, so feel free to split this tap into two parts, using the clearing part when you're feeling a little low and the creating part when you're ready to welcome new opportunities.

Tapping exercise: Part 1 Clear It

SAY IT AND SCORE IT Let's begin with our core self-love affirmation and score how believable it currently feels as a percentage:

I love myself totally, unconditionally and with ease.
Say this affirmation out loud.

Now it's time for the three-step routine: sore spots massage, then notice where you're at on the frequency scale. Notice your posture. Take a deep breath, inhale and exhale.

Now repeat the following, filling in the blanks as appropriate:

When I say, 'I love myself totally, unconditionally and with ease', I feel ...
Because ...
But it is possible for me to love and accept myself anyway.

Each time you use this routine different gremlins, aspects, memories and emotions will arise. Try to pay attention to your body while you tap – where do you feel tension? Remember that your body holds clues for you.

CLEAR IT Tap through the Rapid Tapping points as you say each of the following statements:

- Even though I don't feel fully lovable
- Even though I don't find unconditional value in myself
- Because . . .
- And that makes me feel . . .
- I'm noticing it now
- I'm noticing where my body holds this pain
- It's here in my . . .
- I don't love myself enough, maybe I feel a bit unlovable
- And that's hard for me to admit
- Maybe I've put conditions on the love I can feel for myself
- I often feel like something's wrong with me
- I don't even know why I feel this way, or what I believe to be wrong
- But sometimes I'm mean to myself
- I accept that now
- I am only human
- I don't always choose to love my soul
- But I am an infinite soul and that is incredible.

Inhale and exhale, mindfully. Take a rest, a stretch and a sip of water.

Tap on the collarbones and heart area:

I accept the way I'm feeling right now.
I accept more of myself right now.

Hand on heart. Notice and accept any shift or change that is healing and clearing you.

Let's do a body scan together:

1   Let the compassionate, loving energy flow through you. I invite you to notice your body, to feel your feet and to wiggle your toes. Allow your feet to grow roots and let them sink deep into the earth's core, grounding you.
2   Scan all the way up through your body, up, up, up till you reach your heart, closing your eyes and holding on to your heart, and then moving up to your head. Allow yourself to notice anything in your body that feels tight or represents this feeling of being unlovable and the tension that brings.
3   Now open your eyes and let your wise unconscious self be drawn to the source of tension.

Sore spots massage:

- I have this feeling in my body
- Amazingly, my body is just trying to keep me safe
- I choose to release this now
- It is possible for me to feel safe?
- Maybe I haven't in the past
- But I can feel safe in the future

- But I still have this tension in my body
- This feeling in my body, I honour it, but maybe it's safe to let it go now
- Maybe it's safe to let this pain go
- Maybe it's not safe at all
- My body is good at keeping me safe
- Maybe I can relax
- Maybe I would be OK without this tension
- What if I let this tension go?
- I could choose to release it now
- I will love myself fully, even though I haven't in the past
- I can decide to do this right now
- What if I put no conditions on the love I could feel for myself?
- What if I chose a new way, even if it's scary and unknown?
- I know deep down that I am worthy to choose again
- So I choose again
- I am ready to love myself more right now.

Let this sink in, attune your senses to it. You may not immediately notice the shift in your outlook, but the tapping has already taken effect deep within. Get up, smile, dance, sing a little tune and embrace it: make use of the shifted energy you've invited in. Begin sealing!

HEAD HUG With one hand on the back of your head and one at the front, take a head hug here and hold this position, silently. Breathe intentionally – let things calibrate.

SAY IT

- I honour myself and I choose to love myself
- Any remaining friction in my body, I release into love
- I relax into love
- I smile into love
- I release all my old fear because it is possible for me to love myself unconditionally.

Smile like you mean it. You're lovely. Take both hands and place them on your heart.

SEE IT Close your eyes and visualise something lovely – a special place, a loved one or anything that embodies this word for you. Take your time to adjust and focus on your new surroundings and allow yourself to shift and move into love. Imagine warm, beautiful golden light above you, which pours, almost like honey, through your body and all your cells, through every part of your nervous system. Know that with every moment it is going to replenish you, and fill you up with the love that you require.

SAY IT AND SCORE IT March on your feet and with a smile say to yourself:

I love myself totally, unconditionally and with ease.

Open your eyes and move your body. Now stretch up. Notice how you're feeling. Check in with yourself on the frequency scale. Has your inner love vibration gone up? Does your affirmation now feel more believable to you?

If you want to take a break now, that's totally fine. If you feel ready to start creating, we can move on to the second part of the tap together.

Either way, it's time to affirm the positive energy that you've created, to seal it in. Think of this step as the cling film you would use to keep food fresh, except it's your loving feelings that we're keeping yummy. We are acknowledging the parts of us that are now waking up. We are not held back by stress but are flourishing through love.

Tapping exercise: Part 2 Create It

Rub your hands together briskly and pull them up so that they're in line with your forehead. Feel the energy that you're creating and imagine that this is love. Now pour all this love into yourself as you place your hands on your heart. Yum.

Tap through the Rapid Tapping points:

- I'm ready to raise my love vibration right now!
- What if I decided to fully and unconditionally love myself?
- What would it feel like?
- It would feel good, there is nothing to fear here!
- I choose to love myself, no matter what
- I am worthy and I am enough as I am, every single day
- Even if things go wrong, even if I feel bad and even if I have all these emotions
- I know deep down that I am loved, and I am infinite!

Good. Wonderful. And now we're going to do a quick tap through. And I want you to notice how you're feeling right now. What's come up that feels positive?

Tap with me through the points, adding your positive feeling each time:

- I feel...
- I feel...
- I feel...
- I feel...
- I feel...
- I feel...

Take a breath, let it out. If you feel something to be true, we're going to thymus-thump, as you say out loud:

I am Love
I am Love
I am Love.

Smile. Hold your heart. Shut your eyes. Take a deep breath in. And exhale. Relax and sink into your natural state of love. Smile, move your body, laugh.

SAY IT
It is possible for me to love myself unconditionally!

Now take deep breaths and relax. Reflect on your practice and what you have learnt. Can you take one small intuitive step towards making your vision a reality right now?

THE WHEEL OF POSSIBILITY: RAPID TAPS

I'll now offer daily taps for each zone of the Wheel of Possibility. Think of this as putting the E.M.P.O.W.E.R. method from Chapter 4 into practice. You can revisit these taps as often as you like for an instant pick-me-up. Before providing a rapid tap for each zone of the Wheel, here's a shortened version of the core self-love tap that's perfect for daily use.

Tapping exercise: The Steady Self-love Daily Tap

Place your hands above your heart, take a deep breath in and exhale through your mouth. Now move to the sore spots and say with me:
When I think about loving myself fully, and completely, it can make me feel . . .

Notice how you feel here. There is no right or wrong answer as we all have different relationships with ourselves. Massage the sore spots and try to pinpoint the part of you – however big or small – that *does* love you completely and unconditionally. You're going to tune in to that part of you.

SAY IT
Even though, over the years, I haven't loved myself unconditionally, I choose now, to love myself fully and steadily, no matter what.
Say this affirmation out loud

CLEAR IT Now we're going to overcome some of the blocks that stop you from feeling that true, abundant self-love is possible. Tap through the Rapid Tapping points, breathing mindfully as you do.

- I choose to release all parts of me that remember what it's like not to be loved
- I haven't always loved myself, but right now, right here, I choose to love myself
- No matter what
- I give myself permission, to step into steady self-love
- I am enough, just as I am
- I have nothing to prove, I have nothing I need to do
- That's it
- My soul knows that it is possible for me to love myself
- And all parts of me, right now
- So I choose this.

Now take a break to let your feelings sit with you for a moment. Take a deep breath in as you change and renew, releasing anything that's holding you back as you breathe out. Shake it out, and stand – move about, smile!

SAY IT
It is possible for me to love myself fully and completely.

OPTIONAL EXERCISE What would become possible for you if you step into this frequency? Come up with three benefits for either you or someone close to you. Hold your heart, smile and say:
If I love myself fully and completely, I will be able to . . .

THE ENERGETICS ZONE

Energetics relates to everything that contributes to your energy so your emotions, personality, beliefs, self-image and frequency. It's a bit like the Law of Oneness is to the other Laws of the Universe: it's the mothership of our lives. Get this right, and the rest follows suit.

Tapping exercise: The Positive Vibes Daily Tap

SAY IT AND SCORE IT
Positive vibes.

How true does this statement feel for you? I want you to dig deep and ask yourself if you are truly happy and content, or whether you're willing yourself to be positive and putting on a brave face. If you fall into the latter camp, don't panic, because by the end of this tap we will have raised your overall frequency.

We're going to start with a body scan. Try to quieten the chatter in your mind and focus on how your body feels. Where are you holding tension that's stopping you from fully embracing positive vibes? We're going to home in on these areas to reduce any stagnant energy so that you can step into all the positive vibrations available to you right now.

Rub your hands together as you complete your body scan. Begin at the crown of your head and move down to your heart, all the while taking deep breaths in through your nose and out through your mouth. Once you're ready, you can begin your sore spots massage, and repeat the following statements:

- I choose to release any negative vibes I feel ...
- When I adopt a positive mindset, I feel good ...
- But sometimes things get in the way and blind me from the positives ... (*list what stops you from feeling truly content and positive about your possibilities and potential*)
- I get in my own way because ... (*gently ask yourself why?*)
- Continue to massage your sore spots, as you reflect on what's blocking your way.

SAY IT AND SCORE IT
It is fully possible for me to have more positive vibes now. I decide this for myself, right now.

How true does this statement feel for you now?

CREATE IT What makes you smile? Cast your mind back to a happy, safe memory. Now smile with me as you allow your body to relax. Close your eyes and slowly reach your hands up to the ceiling to mirror your growing positive vibes. Count to three, before placing your hands on your heart. Now, stay here, smile, or laugh if you can.

You should now be feeling a stronger charge in your body. Shake your arms and legs out, before tapping with me on your collarbones and heart area:

- I accept these positive vibes.
- I give myself permission to feel them.
- I choose to remember them.
- I clear and release all the leftover negativity.
- I have the power to decide.
- I accept and receive my most positive state.
- It is safe for me to accept true positivity.
- This is my natural state.

SEAL IT To seal the change in, you want to move about and get a feel for your body again. March on the spot, smile and sing a happy tune if you can.

AFFIRM IT
I am positive – this is my new vibration.

Hold your heart, take a deep breath in, release and hold. Feel the positive vibrations running through your body, from the top of your head to the tips of your toes.

How do you feel post-tap? You should feel a renewed sense of purpose and energy. Make sure to come back to this tap whenever you're feeling a little low and you're in need of a pick-me-up.

THE MONEY ZONE

Money is often tied up with anxiety. We worry constantly about whether we have enough of it, how we can make more of it and what we should use it for. Some of your most immediate thoughts about money will relate back to messages you absorbed growing up, and these can be anything from 'money doesn't grow on trees' to 'money is the key to happiness'. These are two extremes of the spectrum, but you get the picture. To better understand your own attitude towards money, make a list of the things that come to mind when you think about what it means to you. Once you've had a chance to reflect on your list, you're ready to start tapping.

Tapping exercise: The More Money Daily Tap

SAY IT AND SCORE IT
I am making all the money I need, in ways that I enjoy.

Take a moment to consider how true this statement feels for you right now. If your percentage is low, you need to get rid of your negative thought patterns around money, as they're not serving you.

Place your hands on your heart while you say:
It is easy for me to make more money.

How do you feel? Focus on what feelings this statement conjures up as you tap through the Rapid Tapping points.

Now move on to the sore spots massage, as you say:

When I think about inviting more money into my life, it makes me feel ...
Because ...
But it is possible for me to create more money.

CLEAR IT Refer back to the list that you created at the start of the tap, and identify the negative ideas you associate with money. Now say each one out loud as you tap through the Rapid Tapping points again and let go of each one as you do.

CREATE IT It's time to swap out those negative thought patterns and seal in new, positive beliefs around money. Tap through the rapid points for a third time, and focus on the following as you do:

- Money is energy
- It is a currency, just like energy
- It's there to be created and used
- I freely give money
- I freely receive money
- All my creative ideas around money are waking up
- I don't block money any more
- I attract money easily
- Small amounts
- Big amounts
- All is well
- It is fully possible for me to make more money
- It can be used to help people
- I am abundant.

Now hold your heart. Take a deep breath in through your nose and out through your mouth as you recalibrate into this new vibration. End this tap by smiling and acknowledging that money is a resource – and one that's readily available to you.

THE PHYSICAL ZONE

How would you score your physical health? What emotions do you feel right now towards your own health, body image and vitality? This tap is all about making peace with our body and accepting that although it may not be perfect, it is still worthy of our gratitude.

Tapping exercise: The Fall in Love with Your Body Tap

Begin by placing your hands over your heart and taking a couple of deep breaths in and out. Then repeat:
I accept my body the way it is.

Although it might be difficult at first to get the words out, as soon as we accept something and vocalise it, we let go of the tension and energy around it.

Then move on to the sore spots massage, while you say:

I accept my body the way it is
When I think about the aches and pains in my body
It makes me feel . . .
But even though I have these feelings, I choose to accept my body
I choose to love all of me.

Let the words really resonate in your mind and shift
your focus to all the things you love about your body.
Think back to the times that it has protected you and
shielded you.

CLEAR IT Now, it's time to release the negative energy that
you've stored about your body.

- I ask my mind to stop tearing down my body
- I'm sick of feeling this way
- I do not want to feel uneasy in my body
- I may not always feel safe in my body
- But I accept and love myself anyway
- I accept and love myself anyway
- I accept and love myself anyway
- I accept my mind, my body and my soul.

CREATE IT Place your hands over your heart, take deep
breaths in and out. With each inhale focus on the new and
the possible, and with each exhale let go of the old pain and
resentment you hold against your body.

Tap through the Rapid Tapping points and say:

- I know deep down that I have so much power at my
  fingertips
- I decide to focus on health, vitality and love
- I tune in to the parts of me that work in perfect harmony
- I'm so thankful for my body, for working 24/7
- Just for me
- It's time to respect and love my body back now

- It might be tired
- I tune in now to the perfect parts of my being and I am so thankful
- It is fully possible for me to feel better, right now
- I choose to feel better, right now.

Now move into a full body tap – waking up your body, part by part – then go about the rest of your day with a renewed appreciation for your body.

THE 'OOH' ZONE

Whether you're in a long-term relationship, in the throes of something new or you're thinking about getting back into the world of dating, you're probably looking to develop a meaningful bond and an amazing love life, right? Well then, this is the tap for you. It will encourage better vibes in all your relationships, but particularly romantic ones – so let's get started.

Tapping exercise: The Amazing Love Life Tap

Begin by placing your hands on your heart and take a trip down memory lane, reflecting on your past relationships (including the ones that you'd rather forget). Remember to breathe while you do this.

Now move on to the sore spots massage and repeat:

When I think of my love life, I feel ...
Because ...
But I accept and love myself fully.

It might be difficult to give voice to how you truly feel, but, as with all tapping work, you need to dig deep.
I accept that I'm willing to love myself, fully and completely.

Remember: before you can even think about loving someone else, you need to love and appreciate yourself. It all begins with self-love.

CLEAR IT

- An amazing love life starts with me
- I don't always love myself enough and completely
- Maybe my love life hasn't been quite right in the past
- But perhaps an ideal relationship doesn't exist
- Even so, I'm ready for love
- I choose to let go of my negative associations and insecurities when it comes to love
- I am ready for love
- I am worthy
- I am powerful
- I am deserving
- I am enough
- I am ready for love.

Sit and let this sink in for a moment, before moving on to a body scan. How do you feel now – can you feel the positive energy flowing through your body?

Consider this as you continue to tap on your collarbones and heart area:

- What would happen if I loved myself?
- What if I chose to love myself in the way that I so deeply want my relationship to be like?
- This is my new intention around love.

CREATE IT It's time to create the amazing love life that you deserve, so tap with me through the rapid points, as you repeat:

- I deserve an amazing love life
- I choose to put myself first today
- I have decided to love myself, to love everyone around me and to receive love in return
- I am entitled to love
- I am born to love
- I give myself permission to have an amazing, brilliant love life
- This is my intention
- It is fully possible for me
- My first step, the first action, that I will take, is . . .

Now this is where it's over to you. What's the first inspired action you're going to take now you have positively programmed your mindset when it comes to love? What are you going to *do* to bring your vision closer to you? Be open to new possibilities and take risks based on your intuition.

Smile as you really let that sink in. Hold your heart. Breathe.

THE WORK ZONE

Procrastination. Let's admit it, we've all let it get the better of us at one point or another. But if you've got a looming deadline and bills to pay, you can't always afford to 'put it off for just one more day'. This tap will allow you to find the focus, passion and purpose you need to get stuck into any task.

Tapping exercise: The Focused Flow Tap

SAY IT AND SCORE IT
I am easily focused and in flow with my work.

How true does this statement feel for you?

CLEAR IT Let's clear some of the blocks that are stopping you from achieving your potential, as you tap through the rapid points with me:

- I can't do this
- I could be doing more
- I am putting things off
- I'm not productive enough
- I'm lazy

- Or am I too hard on myself?
- Am I holding myself to exacting standards?
- What if I believed I was capable?
- I can take small steps forward
- I can get started
- If I make a start, things will fall into place
- I am capable
- It is within my power.

CREATE IT To match the theme of this tap, we're moving swiftly to creating. Begin with a full body scan, tapping through all the parts of your body, and then move onto the rapid points while you consider the following:

- I fully intend to notice my body now and release this tension
- I feel this emotional attachment in my body (*focus on a specific body part*)
- But I accept this is the way it is right now
- And I love myself anyway
- I'm ready to release tension and get moving
- I will celebrate myself once I get moving again
- I have cleared my mind and I can focus
- I choose to focus on the pleasure of completing the task at hand
- This thought motivates me
- I will open up to a new way of approaching what I need to do
- I welcome fulfilment
- This is my choice
- I am ready right now!

Now, shake it out, move, breathe and smile.

AFFIRM IT
I am easily focused and in flow with my work.

How does this statement feel now?

You may want to go through this tap more than once to seal in your renewed energy and focus, or perhaps you're ready to get cracking straight away!

THE ENVIRONMENT ZONE

This tap is all about welcoming abundance into your life and opening yourself up to opportunity so that you can make your dream lifestyle a reality. Remember, feelings of scarcity and lack are in direct opposition to effective manifestation.

Tapping exercise: The Dream Lifestyle Tap

SAY IT AND SCORE IT Place your hands over your heart and say:
When I think about my lifestyle, I feel ...

Does this conjure up predominantly negative or positive feelings? What percentage are you at when it comes to your lifestyle?

CLEAR IT Begin by massaging the sore spots. Now that you've gained some clarity on how you feel about your current lifestyle, repeat the following statements:

I feel ...
Because ...
But I choose to accept and appreciate what I have.

Notice how your energy changes when you choose to adopt a 'glass half full' mindset. It's important to first focus and celebrate what you do have, before trying to create more. You expand rather than contract. You open rather than close.

SEAL IT As you tap, alternating between your collarbones and heart area, say:

When I think about my lifestyle now, it is possible for me to appreciate and accept where I am.
When I accept and appreciate what I have now, I open my heart to more.

Place your hands on your heart and take a couple of deep breaths. As you do so, gently remind yourself that your dreams and wants are valid. See them as added bonuses to what you already have in your life. There's less pressure to achieve when you're coming from a place of appreciation.

Tapping with me on the rapid points:

- My dream lifestyle is possible
- It doesn't always feel that way, but it's my vision
- It's not going anywhere
- So I choose to tune in to it fully
- In this moment, I choose to accept my own desires
- It's not wrong to want my dreams to come true
- My vision isn't going anywhere.

SEE IT It's time to use your senses to visualise and mentally rehearse what your dream lifestyle looks like. Tap through the rapid points:

- I will put my all into visualising my future
- What do I want from my dream lifestyle?
- How would I feel?
- I can sense the positive energy and I choose to follow it
- I notice how my body feels
- I think I like this new sensation
- Even though it's a little scary
- It's meant to be
- I am receiving a new vibration now
- This is right for me.

Take a moment to be still. Now march your feet up and down on the spot. Imagine there's a recording of your life in your mind, and fast forward to the scene where you're living your dream life. You're watching a life that you've lived. This is what your future holds.

Place your hands on your heart:
It is done.

Repeat this tap every day to bring into focus and manifest your dream lifestyle.

THE RELATIONSHIPS ZONE

With this tap you will learn how to crank up your killer confidence so that you can enjoy fantastic relationships with your friends, families and colleagues – and most importantly with yourself.

Tapping exercise: The Confidence Tap

Start making a list of all the negatives and positives that you associate with the word 'confidence'. Once you've done this, write down what it would mean to you to be able to step into your most unapologetically confident self.

SAY IT AND SCORE IT Now that you've considered what confidence really means to you, say the following sentence aloud:
I feel truly confident and believe in my own power.

How true does this feel for you? If you're not 100 per cent, that's OK. Pause for a moment and think about why this might be. What experiences, interactions and beliefs have affected your confidence?

Massage the sore spots as you repeat:

I feel . . .
Because . . .
But it is possible for me to acknowledge that this is the way it is right now.

And again:

I feel . . .
Because . . .
But it is possible for me to acknowledge that this is the way it is right now.

CLEAR IT Begin by tapping the rapid points, while imagining a version of yourself that's unapologetically confident:

- I feel . . .
- I feel . . .
- I feel . . .

Pick a memory from the past that you feel affected your confidence. This may be difficult to address, so make sure you're ready and in a safe space:

- I remember . . .
- I felt . . .
- I acknowledge that memory but I'm ready to move on
- It's OK
- I'm only human.

Take a deep breath here and exhale:

- I don't feel confident
- And on some level I know that's OK
- But it doesn't feel good
- It's really hard
- Why don't I believe in myself?
- I wonder why that is?
- I wonder why I'm not confident in myself?

As we tap here, close your eyes, ask yourself that question and really feel it in your body as well:
Why am I not confident enough?

Allow the memory to appear in your mind's eye. Sit with it and notice how it makes you feel. I know it's challenging, but please remember that I'm with you and supporting you in spirit.

Now say with me:

- This feeling ...
- I'm just noticing it now
- I can feel it in my body.
- This feeling in my body
- I've been carrying it for so long
- Too long
- This feeling in my body is weighing me down.

Hold your heart. Take a deep breath, and release. Allow your body to relax and now repeat:

- I acknowledge and accept my life
- I decide to love myself anyway

- I release my trapped energy
- I wonder what it would feel like to have that killer confidence.

SAY IT

If I were already fully confident, I would feel . . .

Take a moment here as you tap to notice how you would *feel*.

SEE IT

If I could wave a magic wand and give you confidence, how would your life change? What would it look like? Alternately tap your collarbones and heart area, as you visualise this.

- You are confident
- You are brilliant
- You are powerful.

Now tap through the Rapid Tapping points and move your body with intentional conviction:

- I am confident
- I believe in myself
- I appreciate who I am
- I choose to let go of negative self-talk
- I can be confident too
- I can be more confident than I've ever been before
- I choose to feel able and content

- I have so much to offer
- Maybe it's time to live with this in mind.

Rub your hands together and start to notice the tension in your body dissipate, as you recalibrate.

SAY IT
There is a possibility that I can step into my most confident self.

Does it feel more believable now?

SEAL IT OK, now it's time to seal the positive energy in. Begin by smiling and repeat the following affirmations:

- I choose to feel …
- I choose to feel …
- I choose to feel …
- I am feeling …
- I am feeling …
- I am feeling …
- I feel like this because …
- And I choose every day to love and accept myself fully.

Continue to tap while acknowledging any feelings in your body, however big or small. Lean into this higher frequency. No words are needed for now, just really feel the connection with your body. Think of a colour that feels powerful to you. Imagine that colour spreading through your body.

SCORE IT Now that you're in this energetically attuned state, it's time to check on your frequency again. Has it gone up?

If you still feel some resistance, end with a thymus thump and repeat:

I am confident and I take action!
So go and take that action. Permit self-belief. Repeat, repeat, *repeat* this tap to become your most confident self.

KEEPING IN THE FLOW

Now that you're regularly practising daily tapping routines and in a receptive manifesting state, it's important to learn how to stay in the zone and understand what a 'flow state' is. This is different from adopting a growth mindset – it's more about surrendering to natural energy and using your body's inbuilt reward centre, where a lot of happy chemicals are released. In the flow state – or what I call 'possibility' – you're invincible, unleashed and energised. I'll outline a template for your morning and evening routine that includes tapping with journalling prompts, and physical movement-based suggestions drawn from somatic therapies. I'll use my expertise within global creative media to help you access ideas that don't come from inside of us at all, but from the flow state inside superconsciousness.

WHAT IS FLOW STATE?

Through tapping you've seen how you can shift your energy to connect to a more positive state of self. You may have glimpsed a flow state where time disappears and you feel like you're in some other kind of tingly place, even joy. You might experience a natural kind of buzz or high from your continued tapping, especially towards the end of the routines I've shared in Part Two. If not, don't worry – just keep tapping and surrender to something bigger than you.

I would recommend tapping into any underlying resistance because it's not always immediately easy to slip into the flow state – if it was, we'd all be at it. If you want to massively increase your performance, your ability, your concentration and your level of engagement, you want the flow state. If you have experienced this altered state with your tapping it's definitely a good thing: neuroscience tells us that we are rewarded with an increase in activity of dopamine (a brain chemical involved in pleasure and motivation), serotonin (which regulates your mood) and endorphins (our natural pain blockers, releasing us a feeling of euphoria) – much like when you've finished a session at the gym. When I run big group workshops at festivals I want to make the crowd feel euphoric, and to do that I help them access their own flow state with tapping!

I believe that when we are in flow we can access the divine superconsciousness, where lots of information – previously inaccessible to us – is suddenly downloadable. In this state I have had business ideas flow out of me in areas I've never considered myself to be knowledgeable in (like a full-on tech idea) – and outlandish television ideas have been commissioned, against all the odds (one of them, *Time Crashers*, was a bizarre idea mixing history and reality, yet was rated highly by the critics). Entire chapters of this book have come from somewhere 'other' than my conscious mind. It's a state that is other-worldly, but even so you might feel completely switched on, focused and together. That's why I call it possibility. Nothing feels totally impossible here.

> *'I think that ideas exist outside of ourselves. I think somewhere, we're all connected off in some very abstract land. But somewhere between there and here ideas exist.'*
> DAVID LYNCH, film director

This whole flow state – what David Lynch calls the 'very abstract land' – is continually accessible with tapping: that exciting state that Dr Joe Dispenza calls becoming a 'nobody' because we are, for some moment, taken away from the constraints of our body and the chatter of our mind.

Hungarian psychology pioneer Mihaly Csikszentmihalyi gives a legendary TED talk on flow. He explains that flow is a state of complete immersion in any one thing. It's pure focus, away from time and space:

> *'. . . and that when we are in passion or purpose we are more successful and happier. The ego falls away. Time flies. Every action, movement, and thought follows inevitably from the previous one.'*

Csikszentmihalyi explains that we can't understand two people talking at the same time because we don't have the attention for it neurologically, but when we are in flow state we feel our body disappear because our attention is channelled, 'our reality is temporarily suspended'. This is different from relaxation because we are the opposite of bored – we're in sheer focused bliss. We access ideas away from the usual everyday processing. It's effortless. It's graceful. It's non-resistant. It's accepting. It's true. It's pure presence upon presence. It's flow.

Dawson Church refers to this as the 'bliss brain'. Church believes that it's what mystics call a supernatural knowing state, what Christians call being drenched with the Holy Spirit, what Buddhists call a state of enlightenment. Again, it doesn't matter what you call it; the point is that it's accessible to you. And it's the most real thing you've ever felt. If you've experienced it, the clock time that exists, the imps, the fear goblins and the inner critics all tend to shut up and instead you bask in a deep sense of truth. Truth of consciousness.

Like everything else you've learnt, in order to consolidate your flow, it's useful to repeat and reinforce it. Simply tap more so you get used to this being a normal thing for you. This flow state is what I refer to as the 'sealing in' process at the end of most of the Rapid Tapping routines, when you shift up the frequency scale towards that bliss feeling. It's so important to take time just enjoying the wonderful moment you have created, that moment of miraculous possibility that exists within yourself. But it goes further than simply affirming this at the end of your taps. You can embody this frequency by fostering a set of energy-fuelling techniques too, like meditation, journalling, music-frequency healing and visualisation.

HOW TO STAY IN FLOW

There are many ways to open up your energy channels to this flow state – it all depends on which you feel led to. As well as tapping, you can explore chakras, yoga, crystals, qi gong, creative writing, art, music, deep meditation or anything that feels like it's tapping you into a creatively inspiring space that allows you to escape a sense of day-to-day drudgery.

I love Hal Elrod's book *The Miracle Morning* and recommend it to my clients. Sharing my bugbear about clock time, he advises waking up one hour earlier than usual so you never give 'I haven't got time' as an excuse. He advocates a system called Life S.A.V.E.R.S.: silence, affirmations, visualisation, exercise, reading and scribing. I encourage certain aspects of this below in my morning and evening routine templates, which I'd love to share because to stay in manifesting flow you need to get into the *daily* way of keeping it a lifestyle choice.

So, for fully embodying morning and evening routines to truly consolidate your ongoing tapping work, here's what I recommend:

MY RISE AND SHINE MORNING ROUTINE

Max version: 1 hour
Lite version: 10 minutes

- Wake up an hour earlier than you usually do (yes DO IT!)
- Sit in silence, without your phone or any distractions

- Use the rapid clearing routine to start your day with focus and flowing energy
- Morning journal flow
- Body activation: Do your stretching, qi gong, yoga, pilates or gentle cardio exercise
- Use the rapid creating routine
- Read or listen to something inspiring like a podcast (mine?!) and try some brain-boosting, awakening tunes and beats such as binaurals or solfeggios
- Visualise your day ahead in positive terms – go through what is possible for you and FEEL it by connecting with each of your senses and moving your body.

SWEET DREAMS EVENING ROUTINE

Max version: 1 hour
Lite version: 10 minutes

- Get ready for bed an hour earlier than you usually do, or carve out an hour of alone time (DO IT!)
- Light candles, smell scents and invest in lovely nightwear that makes you feel good
- Body activation: do some stretching, qi gong, gentle yin yoga, yoga nidra, breathwork or a calming exercise for your body to zone down
- Use the rapid clearing routine
- Practise sleep manifestation or do a guided sleep tap with me (audio or video)
- Evening journal flow

- Re-visualise your day, editing it in the way you'd prefer it to have happened
- Positively visualise the best things that could happen tomorrow.

Feel free to switch these routines up and tweak them so that they feel good for you. I have seen some clients do this across three hours and pop in all sorts of mindful moments of their own, experimenting with online courses or gardening. I like to play music and meditate as well as routinely bathe with oils and salts. Enjoy it!

Note If you're thinking, yeah – sounds nice – but I can't possibly do this – then you *really* need to find the time and just start. I have one client called Cait, a single mum of three young children, who works ten-hour daily shifts as a matron with the NHS – if she can find the time each morning, so can you. It's a question of taking that first baby step, starting with maybe just ten minutes earlier on the alarm and gradually building it up. Trust me, it will get addictive in a good way! Your soul is starving for this 'me-time'. But there's more. The cumulative effects of daily tapping are far-reaching and Cait's extra tap time has allowed her to set up a successful side hustle as a yoga teacher, because she's been able to tap on procrastination, resistance and fear of change.

Cait says, 'Rapid Tapping has been truly transformational. I started using it during times of stress, anxiety and low mood, but I immediately started feeling the benefits. It has completely changed my energy for the better. I've gained confidence in myself, I've used tapping for goal-setting and I've even started a new business while building up my self-worth and self-love. I now believe that anything is possible for me because it is!'

10 READY AND PRIMED FOR ACTION

We're almost there! While you've been playing detective on your own life through the theory and practice outlined in this book, now is the time to amplify what you've learned by getting out there and *doing*.

Many traditional Law of Attraction followers would tell you that you don't need to take any action at all; that your aspirations will just manifest if you keep thinking about them in a positive way. This is far-fetched. We live on this planet, in these bodies – and there is a certain set of structures in place that we need to adhere to. However, there is a middle ground and a sweet spot for effective and rapid manifesting. Just as we can't hold back and spend all day meditating and visualising our way to the version of life success and fulfilment we are after, neither can we force it to happen.

I go deep into this in my own seven-stage manifesting process, Pivot into Power, which draws on ancient wisdom, coaching frameworks and new science to empower you to manifest your desires into tangible 'done deals' using tapping. I'm going to offer a brief outline here so you can bear the process in mind when manifesting:

Desire: What do you desire in life? Break down your big dreams into more manageable desires.

Discover: Now ask yourself what forms the basis of your desire.

Decide: You've decided that this is possible for you.

Debunk: This one's the biggie – and tapping is your best friend here. Debunk everything that's holding you back and telling you your desire isn't possible.

Ditch: Consider what needs ditching and let go of your ruthless productivity. Don't confuse familiarity with happiness. Let go of the things, people and places that don't serve you.

Do: It's time to take inspired action. In this stage of the process we make it happen.

Done: This is the trickiest stage of my manifesting process – surrendering to the idea that on some level what you want to accomplish is already done.

One of the big teachings I want to share is using the power of intention. Before all action I ask myself: what is my intention? What is the outcome I am looking for? Don't power ahead before you can answer these questions. Intention is the energetic rocket fuel behind what you want, whereas goals are your end result destination. There's a subtle but important difference here. Trudging doggedly towards a goal for the goal's sake alone, while making sure you get it at all costs, is not the same frequency as pulling that goal towards you. Becoming, feeling and having what we want involves actionable change – but are you willing to embrace that? Accomplished manifestors know that becoming a 'puller' is more productive than pushing, and I'll explain why in this important chapter.

'Our intention is everything. Nothing happens on this planet without it. Not one single thing has ever been accomplished without intention.'

JIM CARREY, actor

Here are key questions for you to journal on and think about if you want to get intentional:

- Why do you want to pivot into this outcome?
- What energy qualities are you bringing to your daily and longer-term actions?
- Will you want this when the work gets difficult?
- How are you acting according to your heart, your intuition *and* your head knowledge – or are you just thinking with your head and ignoring your inner guidance?
- If I waved a magic wand and you were offered what you want right now, would you be ready to take it?
- Are you making excuses or using blame? Are you hoping that what you want will pop up out of nowhere without any action on your part, as if by magic?
- Are you subscribing to the 'hustle harder' mentality that is at odds with your nervous system? There's a two-way conversation going on when we want to create something. It's a co-creation experience and we need to act upon the nudges, the hunches and the whispers of our heart as well as get down and dirty with willpower. After all, we live on Earth, not in the sky.

So this is the chapter that inspires you to get grounded and strategic about taking inspired action to kickstart (and then maintain) your new life of infinite possibilities.

PUSHING V. PULLING

Having worked through this book you'll now be aware of the ripple effect that your own transformation can have on others around you. When you woke up this morning and used your journal or tapped, you probably had no idea that during the day you made a choice that set someone off on an entirely different course of action. Even smiling at someone could make all the difference. If you're still thinking you might not matter as much as someone else (which isn't true) then how about considering all your actions from now on as a way to shine light on other people? You don't have to be a world-changer to change the world. You'll do it in your own way. Just as tapping shifts your energy over time and with consistency can radically transform your entire view on life, so can your choice of words, behaviours and actions transform the lives of others (and most certainly those you love) TODAY. So, to close the book, I'll explain how you can use your new power to empower others – to step out into the world and take action that counts.

We begin by noticing our societal love affair with hard work, determination and pushing. By her own admission these qualities got one of my clients, Karen Howes, unquestionably far in life. She founded and runs one of the most respected luxury design studios in the UK, Taylor Howes Design, is a mother of two and a charity fundraiser. Overseeing a team of forty employees, Karen has worked on everything from restoring ancient palaces to designing 18,000-square-foot luxury new builds. But, in line with this scale of success and hard work, comes the natural fallout of her occasional burnout and exhaustion-induced anxiety. She must develop new skills and techniques to enter a busy working week – something she's not accustomed to – but tapping has enabled Karen to remove limiting beliefs and manage stress.

'Start by doing what is necessary, then what is possible, and suddenly you are doing the impossible.'

ST FRANCIS OF ASSISI

It is important to make the first move and question if you need very necessary time off. A bit of gritty determination and some all-nighters planning your successes can be necessary at the start of any goal, but then what? Our bodies, as we know, can't carry on that way forever.

What's next? What can I do? How can I slow down? I hear these voices inside my own head. The pusher inside is angling us to stay pushing because it knows what that feels like. It's back to the brain again, searching through and finding old evidence to back up the fact we should be running on high adrenalin and addictive stress hormones. Adrenal fatigue is body depletion and energetic overload; it's not a badge of honour. In order to switch gears to a slower pace, we require some seriously hard evidence to prove to us that doing less doesn't necessarily equal less success. We need to take action and shift into another realm, and begin 'pulling' instead.

What's a pusher?

If you're a pusher you're essentially chasing your tail. You might be scrolling obsessively around social media; you might be checking everything twice. You might be putting everyone first but you're not stopping to take adequate self-care. You're 100 miles an hour, but little is actually getting *done*. You're visualising the worst-case scenario most of the time, which means that you're being negative towards yourself all the time. You probably love to-do lists – and maybe you even secretly love the seduction of keeping going until you're exhausted, because it means you've worked hard, and working hard means success.

After a while you get into desperation mode. And you might send five more emails in this pent-up state, and your internal dialogue might sound something like, 'Then I'll do it, then that will work, maybe that will help, I should stay up until I finish this.' You might work even though in the state you're in your output will be below par. Or you will try desperately to make rigid plans. And there's no question – you're a real doer, you might be really good at doing vision work, self-development, plans – but then you want to stick to it. You want results. You're like, what will make me get this NOW? You're thinking about strategy and how you get to where you want to be all the time. What is the plan? How is the strategy going? What can I learn? Maybe I can do a course on that, or maybe I can do a qualification on that? But then you've overloaded yourself. So you start getting angry with yourself again, right? It's a vicious cycle of self-flagellation. You're always on the hunt for 'the next thing'; being exactly where you are feels odd to you. Usually, a pusher suffers with comparison-itis too. You're constantly looking at what everyone else is doing. And you immediately think, I'm not as good.

I've just described pushers who might have a to-do list on the go, so maybe you're thinking 'Oh phew, doesn't sound like me', but you can also be at the other end of the spectrum and be a super-scattered pusher. No plan, but you're throwing spaghetti at the walls all the time, right? You're hoping something sticks. You might often zone out. When you're not working or doing something, you're doing very little, but you're into vices, you're craving holidays, you're numbing out, you might be prone to addiction or extreme highs and lows. And you are not happy deep down because you're not *living*, in your opinion. This can't be it, can it? And you tend to have a fixed mindset about stuff you can do. I can do it, or I can't do it. You say stuff on repeat all the time. Your self-talk is off the scale.

I'm exhausted just writing this.

Most people are natural pushers. We just get into habits, which are actual neurological pathways, which are then reinforced and ingrained as familiar. And what does our brain do? It filters, it looks for the familiar. And it says, 'I know this, OK, I know this feeling.' But you are in perpetual stress and anxiety, so you're not receiving all the love, possibilities and opportunities out there. You're not seeing the miracles or noticing the synchronicities when taking action, because you're going through the motions of the past.

That's a pusher. If you are one, then your action is too strong, and you're embodying a distressed mania that keeps your action yielding lower results. Yes, you'll do well but you are trying to do it on pure willpower – just imagine what you could do if you become more of a puller.

So what's a puller?

If you keep tapping and using the techniques here you can be in pusher recovery (like me) and switch into being a puller. Or maybe you are already a puller and you can upgrade into even more of a receiver, like I do every month by doing this work over and over again, looking at different life zones to make them whole and healed into abundance.

A puller will methodically stand their ground and take time for themselves. They will notice that self-care is good and necessary and non-negotiable, diarising time for both creative pursuits and alone-time. They enjoy alone-time because they no longer fear the shadows of themselves, but love themselves deeply and completely. They won't look for lost parts of themselves in other people. A puller will feel energetically balanced most of the time because they're doing their internal work and open to changes. They're taking self-development seriously but they're not doing it to 'fix themselves', only to access more of themselves. They're taking daytime breaks, not just breaks at the end of a busy period. And they're honouring their body.

If you're a puller you are innately visualising what you do want, and what you're capable of. You're visualising things as done deals – your self-talk says, 'Yeah, that's possible for me', and you really mean it. You're curious about what's next, not hung up on it. You're OK with change but you're accepting of what can't change. You realise that things are not going to be exactly as we plan them to be in our very limited minds because you know we're in the fabric of the universe, which truly supports you. You're rational about your action: your mindset says, 'Things might not go my way; it's OK though.' You have likely built resilience, because you want to accept change and growth no matter if that has some bumps and setbacks.

You are often called lucky. People may say, 'Wow, you are lucky, aren't you, you've done well.' But you know it isn't luck; you're focusing on what could be, and developing a positive, flexible mindset. So you see everything as experience rather than success or failure. The past is pure experience. It's knowledge and this makes you feel truly powerful at a core level. So you will roll with the punches.

You have a good ability to separate emotion from events. You can witness yourself, and see that all experiences are inherently neutral, but that the meaning we place on them isn't. That's not to say you're a pushover; you're strong and you don't go around tolerating the toxic people in your life. You have solid boundaries. You will try to move away from and debunk the low-frequency emotions that keep you trapped and caged from a particular event. And to do this, the puller will take time to tap and create space for more positive beliefs and habits to emerge, even if it's difficult.

As a puller you will double up on things in a smart and steady way. You might read inspiring books on journeys – nothing is wasted – and you will notice signs and synchronicities and start to work just little by little into harmony with what's coming your way. And essentially, you will emit a magnetic frequency that is a good energy. People want to hang around you – they're drawn to you because you're a puller.

Have you heard of London Fashion Week, or the British Fashion Council, or the Fashion Awards? Well, Caroline Rush CBE is the woman in charge of all this. Caroline has used my vision system, and when defining her vision board and values I was struck at how she's a brilliant example of a puller. She puts in the groundwork, then lets it all happen. She's detailed and excellent at what she does, she never misses a beat, and yet always exudes a sense of calm. We call her The Swan, gliding into her goals like a swan on smooth water, and yet we know those legs and feet under the surface have created the initial and necessary momentum to glide. If something goes wrong on her watch, you also know she won't hesitate to spring into action.

So the one thing to focus on as you create any action steps – big or small – is not to push *all the time*. You can start taking on the behaviours and habits of a puller today by identifying a puller in your life, and noticing how they operate.

When faced with a decision, or when you're taking your action steps, ask yourself, *what would a puller do?* Asking this question and changing your relationship with your action is going to be the very best strategic action plan that you will ever make.

HOW TO GET PULLED

If you can't find a puller to emulate, do the following to help you become a puller and take control back into your life:

- Tap more regularly, focusing on resistance, letting go and surrendering your inner control freak.
- Revert to your vision, and look at your vision board, if you've got one – is it what you see around you yet? Do you feel how you want to feel in that vision? If not, channel your superman/woman 'doer', pushing energy to do something about making *that* happen instead while you continue to tap. The law of perpetual energy in motion tells us that we can redirect negative energy into something worthwhile, so lay off the career, perhaps, and focus on the life zones that require you to mobilise pushing energy.
- Go away and recalibrate. Anywhere, but preferably somewhere where you can have a digital detox and turn off screens and reconnect with your heart.
- Follow reiki, qi gong, meditation, any form of exercise or quiet soothing practices to encourage brain rest and create a new pattern of body slowdown.
- Take time alone – when was the last time you really spent time with yourself and did something just for you?

- Get a pet. Research shows you live longer and happier lives if you have a furry friend. I feel it helps me stay in the 'now' more.
- Hire a professional puller to coach or mentor you – and keep yourself out of that pusher vibe.
- Have more orgasms. Go on.
- Dance. Swear. Be silly and naughty. Play with your time. See what changes.

When we're thinking about adopting the habits of a puller and transforming our pushing mindset, we also need to be conscious of the kind of action we take – is it just plain old boring action or *inspired* action?

ACTION V. INSPIRED ACTION

There are two types of action: there's action, and then there's *inspired* action.

Action is defined as 'the fact or process of doing something, typically to achieve an aim'. It is simply 'a thing done; an act'. This could be a task like personal admin, booking a taxi, driving from A to B, painting a door, food shopping, dropping off your kids somewhere, clearing out a cupboard, completing an important piece of work to a deadline: it's just got to be done.

Inspired action is basing your action on inspiration and intuition, which is 'more about being guided and motivated to do something'.

Creativity, as we now know, is in us all. It is the intuitive part of us longing to be heard and the part that's raw and naive in us. Sometimes we falsely assume this is the part of us that hasn't grown up. But true manifestors know that it must never be quashed.

HACK: Mental stimulation is often numbed because we are plagued with the emotional rollercoaster of life's responsibilities and stresses. When we continue to tap, we calm our nervous system and access flow state, so we can look at things differently and drive our actions more strategically towards joy.

You can use a piggyback approach here. Driving from A to B doesn't need to be just driving. It doesn't need to involve heavy sighing when a car pulls out, or road rage. It can become an inspired action if we decide it is. You could play loud music and say affirmations, entering a euphoric flow state, or you could think up five things you have accomplished and take some time to congratulate yourself and smile in the car. For example, you could notice the benefit of your trip to the shops and be grateful for what it might provide for someone else in your life (like lovely food to eat when they get home).

When you look at the difference between action and inspired action in this way, the former feels even more like drudgery and the latter like a flash of brilliance.

You can turn any action into inspired action just by questioning your motivation behind any given task. It sounds obvious – but what is *motivating* you to do what's on your to-do list? From the following list identify what motivates *you* specifically at the moment. Get to grips with what is making you get up each day and what you want more of:

- Achievement
- Advancement
- Autonomy
- Financial reward
- Impact
- Personal or spiritual growth
- Recognition
- Responsibility

See if you can order these from one (being the most important) to eight (being least important).

To help you decide, I recommend a little trick. Pretend you are asked to interview someone and need to find out what motivates *them*. What questions would you ask? Probably things like: What do you do spontaneously in your spare time? What do you talk about with friends and family? Where do you put your energy? Now just ask yourself the same questions and interrogate yourself.

Got your list of eight motivating factors? Now do more of the stuff you give a shit about. Delegate or ditch the actions you find uninspiring.

And of course, you can change your mindset about *any* task by tapping on it, reframing it and seeing it differently. It's your choice.

Now you know about motivating factors, here's another hack you can use around making lists. As you create your various life action lists, think about what you will now change in your life, take time to go through each element on your 'do' list and make each thing as inspired as you can. Whether it is a daily action list (aka to-do list) or a longer-term action list (aka a visionary game plan), you can inject it with positive intention using a few simple steps.

How to make an inspired action list

Here's an **action** list:

- Go to the dentist
- Take my pet to the vet to get his jabs
- Do the accounts
- Buy food for my son's birthday party
- Fill in that form for work
- Go to the gym for a pilates class
- Send those emails.

Snooze alert. That's just a bland set of actionables.
Now look at *this* **inspired action** list:

- Go to the dentist because my teeth are going to look much better
- Take my pet to the vet to get his jabs because I love him and he provides so much joy in my household
- Do the accounts because I am so happy and grateful to have money in my bank account
- Buy food for my son's birthday party because he's someone I am raising to be a kind, caring young man who fills me with joy
- Fill in that form for work because it will help me create more impact in my sphere
- Go to the gym for a pilates class because my body is a divine vessel and I am worth it
- Send those emails because it will bring me more calm and help me reach my wildest goals.

Me please – I'll be you for the day. Can you see the difference?

There's that magic word **'because'** again. Litter this word all over your action plans, to-do lists, Post-it notes, Christmas lists. You're already using it in your tapping. Why? Because it makes things happen faster. The inspired action list is packed with reasons, both logical and emotional. It makes more sense and it lights you up when you read it. It's more like a 'gratitude list meets to-do list' and it allows you to tap into an energy of inspiration. There is meaning behind each action. Boring tasks become soulful steps in the right direction. Each action clearly relates to a bigger overarching goal: your life vision. Every small action counts if you create a list like this.

YOUR TO-DO LISTS ARE A THING OF SELF-TORTURE

I don't like this outdated and addictive concept, and I don't encourage my clients to create to-do lists. Instead I offer some alternatives like using a quadrant list where you divide a page into four sections and mindfully assess a task as either Important, Unimportant, Urgent or Not Urgent. This reduces the inbuilt desire to make our action lists too long. Remember too that the term 'action list' implies the difference between simply doing something like a robot and acting upon a good reason or intention. Stop saying 'to-do list'. The energy here is that is has to happen, it must be done, it's not yet happened, it's a frequency of 'not yet done'; whereas if you are going to become tapped into the super-manifesting side of yourself you want to start using every chance you get to slip into the energy of 'it's done *already*'.

Here's what I mean by this. To manifest your life more effectively, swap your to-do lists for what I call a to-done list.

Using a to-done list

Using this positive approach will do your overall psyche, as well as your energetic frequency, a ton of good. This is the smart antidote to the negative pressure that your ever-increasing to-do list brings to your energy, quietly zapping away at you all the time. You can, at the end of each day, simply insert what you've DONE. This encourages self-respect and self-congratulation; instead of bemoaning what you *haven't* done, you can feel good about what you've already achieved, and set yourself up for more positive, motivating action the next day. The trick here is to start with **my** so you take mental ownership of what you've done. You also swap the *because* (it's already done so you don't need to labour why you've done it) for **and it makes me feel . . .**

Example of a to-done list:

- **My** email to Sarah, outlying my objectives for the company – **and it makes me feel** accomplished.
- **My** decluttered wardrobe is now ordered – **and makes me feel** happy.
- **My** son's laundry is up to date – **and it makes me feel** calm.
- **My** new website is now up and running – **and it makes me feel** like I've started my business so I'm feeling in a better place and more prepared.
- **My** dog has gone to the vet to have his jabs – **and it makes me feel** more loving.

It's a fabulous and speedy way to pause, prioritise and reinforce your positive emotions at the end of every day. You don't need to cold turkey your old to-do list habit – which should be more bearable now that you've discovered the inspired action list method – but how about constructing a to-done list alongside it?

Using the 'my' to begin your to-done actioned items transforms their energy – this is a mini-celebration, however small, of you taking ownership of your action-based achievements as part of your wider manifestation strategy. Over time you will notice the emotions you write down – 'calm', 'happy' and so on – are the ones that you crave and value. This is an indication of what will work for you as a 'seal-in' or affirmation.

For extra oomph:

- Create your to-done list throughout the day, as you would noting down an action or task you need to remember, and use this formula to state your wins
- Say three of them out loud and tap your collarbones and heart as you seal each one in
- Notice the feeling and emotion you record at the end of your achieved task and create your own affirmation out of it, then tap it in!
- Smile like you mean it; when you smile at the same time as celebrating a win, your brain signals happy hormones and speeds up your manifesting.

Manifest with your to-done deal list

You can also extend my to-done list formula and create a personal to-done list for wider goals, like your envisioned future, by creating a 'to-done deal' list.

This is exciting and new. You'll use this technique by 'tapping in' your true state at the end of a Rapid Tapping routine, when you're in a positive, flow state. Your intention is that this 'deal' has been done, signed, sealed, delivered in a parallel universe somewhere (you're ticking it off as a job well done in some other possible realm in another space and time – that's the quantum bit). Your intention as you create this list is to match the same 'done' energy you bring to a real-live 'ticked off the list' to-done item. You don't waste your time worrying about whether it happened: you *know* and *believe* it. It's not a wishful energy.

Example of a to-done deal list:

- **My** house by the sea – **is a done deal because** it is a wonderful place to raise a family **and it makes me feel** so happy and calm.
- **My** promotion at work – **is a done deal because** it empowers me to help more people **and it makes me feel** more ready to start my own business.
- **My** relationship with my new partner – **is a done deal because** I deeply give and receive love **and it makes me feel** cherished each day.

So, to go super advanced here, you can swap to the past tense. Being in a positive frequency post-tapping is the perfect time to believe this: you are embodying the truth that it is yours already (rather than it being a future aspiration linked to an action). You're more likely to stop second-guessing yourself – and you'll feel a bit more inner peace when you think about your future if you keep this up. Remember to keep your list expansive but not fantastical.

For extra oomph:

- Visualise each item on your to-done deal list with all your senses. How does it feel to be in your house by the sea? What are you wearing, what can you hear and what is it like to see yourself living there? Focus on the feeling and tap on it as you recall a memory that takes you back there.

- Start marching on your feet (right leg, then left leg) as you say your to-done deal list out loud as you tap it in using any points you like here. When you're finished, use a soothing head hug to anchor in the belief that it has happened by connecting you to the emotion, installing healthy happy vibes.
- Smile when you do this to release the good hormones.

THE BASICS OF INSPIRED ACTION

All these techniques are advanced and exciting and practical, but the foundational, non-negotiable *basics* need to be maintained to up-level your life. It's when I don't have these things accounted for that I get the bad moods, that 'dragging-heel' mentality, procrastinate and lack belief around something being possible for me.

How many do you already consider to be non-negotiable (and do you actually do them?)?

- Stay hydrated: studies tell us you'll become moody and more anxious if you don't
- Ensure a nutritious diet; nurture the vessel you have here
- Avoid toxic people and situations wherever possible; they stop you from accessing flow state
- Tap every day: why wouldn't you?
- Journal at least once a day, every day, in an efficient way using my morning and evening journal flows – because you're statistically more likely to do something if you write it down.

- Use gentle stretching, micro-movements, pilates or qi gong each day to move the body, awaken your energy system and restore correct energy balance and flow.
- Smile every day in front of the mirror and say a true affirmation from the end of one of your taps, because you're responsible for loving yourself unconditionally now.

Over to you …

I wrote this book to motivate you, inspire you and connect you to infinite possibilities that exist right now for you to tap into. You've learned and unlearned; you've started clearing and creating; you've resonated and released. The transformative power of tapping is real and you're equipped with techniques and exercises that will guide you to be the most authentic, aligned person you can be so you can manifest more of what you want.

So, what's next? Now it's up to you. I can't take that leap for you, but I do know you will be divinely supported. I do know that you're tapping in, more and more each day – to who you are and what you're capable of. Whatever you're looking to manifest, you're ready.

So I'll keep this simple.

Tap with me on your heart as you say:

It *is* possible for me

(Because it is).

GLOSSARY

Baseline frequency In Rapid Tapping this is an indicator of your unique mindset, your emotions and your manifestations at any given time. We have these barriers or 'set points' in our capacity to feel frequencies of joy, love and ecstasy for ourselves and others. Tapping smashes through these, optimising our overall state.

Body scan When you 'scan' with focus and curiosity through your body in order to connect with your energy and physical condition.

Chasing pain As we release stagnant energy, pain moves. We don't need to be afraid of it, or force it to go away completely; rather we can follow it around the body as we use tapping.

Clear When we intend to reduce, unhook, detach and dissolve emotional and energetic blocks that we do not want.

Conscious mind The tiny 'thinking' part of us (5 per cent) that is conscious, active and known.

Create When we want to implant new energy and positive emotions in order to raise our frequency to manifest what we want.

Drop When you have been waiting for things to 'drop into place' and your intuition aligns – things make sense, as if by magic, all at once when you experience 'the drop'.

Dwell state What we focus on most. Is it in the plus or minus area on the Frequency Scale? Get into the plus area as much as you can with tapping.

Epigenetics the study of how your behaviour and environment can result in changes that affect the way your genes are expressed, without altering your DNA sequence.

Finger tapping Using your thumbs, tap on the inner side of each finger for about five seconds per finger in sequence over and over with a light pressure. Very good when you need to be discreet with your tapping, such as on public transport or in a Zoom meeting.

Frequency Our state of energetics: the energy level we emit to the world, which is defined by our feelings, is how we manifest, so we pay particular attention to raising our frequency with tapping.

Hi-life The highest possible life that embodies all of your true, authentic values with a clear vision and accompanying matching energy.

Human energy The amount of physical and emotional energy we bring to each moment, separate from Universal Energy. Human energy is finite, as are we. We don't need to exist purely on this – we can tap into a lot more.

Impossibility factors When factors in your life have given you unique evidence that it is more impossible than possible, so you dwell more on this.

Journalling Writing down on paper what we feel so we can become aware of subconscious and conscious limitations or self-defeating beliefs. In Rapid Tapping we use daily journalling with a vision to connect our brain and soul to our body, mind and soul in the future as if it is happening now or has happened already.

Lag The place between our conscious thinking and tapping into the superconscious state. When we are overthinking, or not using our intuition, we can feel frustrated and this is 'the lag'.

Laughter When we create spontaneous laughter in Rapid Tapping.

Mindfulness Getting into the 'here and now'; getting into the *now*. Noticing the feeling, in your mind and your body. Acknowledging and honouring the feelings and body sensations.

Mirror neurons Picking up on someone else's feelings or copying without realising; thinking an emotion is your own when it's someone else's, and vice versa.

Negative affirmations Unconsciously or consciously using limiting self-talk or negative everyday language to affirm what you don't want.

Perception Your awareness level depends on how you have uniquely experienced the world so far. This perception is not always to be trusted as it depends on your own upbringing and experiences. What if you tuned into the superconscious (your own intuition) more than this and challenged basic perception?

PMT (Pre-Manifestation Tension) When you're on the road to manifesting your wildest goals, but lots of unpleasant clues that feel like 'tests' from the universe rear their heads and need to be dealt with.

Positive affirmations An affirmation or statement that has a positive outcome without any negative language.

Positive rant Transforming a negative rant into a positive one by switching into ranty gratitude to create an upwards spiral (as opposed to a negative spiral).

Possibility The quantum place where all possibilities exist in a paradigm we can tap into and experience in our reality. Also see Superconscious.

Rapid Tapping points Usually in the following continuous sequence:

- Sore spots massage
- Between eyebrows
- Side of eyes
- Under eyes (use a fluttery, lighter pressure here)
- Under nose
- Chin

- Collarbones and heart
- Additionally:
- Crown/top of head
- Hands on heart
- Thymus thump
- Head hug

Sore spots massage When you massage on the 'sore spots' which are located about two inches down from your collarbones and run across your whole chest. It creates self-connection. Many tapping routines begin with massage here, with a medium pressure, before moving on to the Rapid Tapping points.

Hands on heart Putting both hands, one on top of the other, on your heart and pausing to breathe.

Thymus thump When you 'Tarzan thump' on your upper chest with both fists when saying a true affirmation. This is a quick way to activate your thymus gland, also called the happiness point or spot because it's linked to vitality, immunity and happiness. This energy technique is best known to neutralise negative energy and boost the immune system.

Head hug/Head hold The head hug or head hold, usually used after a seal-in: hold one hand over your forehead and the other over the back of your head to soothe and seal in a desired energy.

Seal-in The part within a tap where you experience a positive shift in your energy and emotions and want to seal it and anchor it in. Often accompanied by a smile or movement to embody the flow and correct balance of energy. This tells your body it is a fact; use it and take inspired action at this point.

Shadow The part of us that we want to keep hidden away, try to minimise or do not admit to having.

Subconscious mind The 95 per cent mainframe from where we manifest, make decisions, go away from or towards a goal. It's a blueprint from our past, locked in as a way to navigate life from our own experience and perceptions. It's the powerhouse of our inner world.

Superconscious The Whole. The I Am. The Everything. The Done. Pure flow. The field of infinite energy. The entire paradigm we belong to and don't access enough, but which is away from time and space in a quantum possibility level.

True affirmations These arise when you have experienced a 'shift' and want to 'seal in' a particular state within a tapping routine, or when a positive affirmation feels over 80 per cent real, believable and possible for you.

Unconscious The deepest level of the subconscious. Shadowed away often; the longest thread from the conscious. Can even carry imprints from generations. However, this is your friend and is all-knowing and wise, working for your highest good.

Universal Energy This is infinite and never dies. Our own energy can be medically measured outside our physical or 'human' energy as a 'field'. It's what we are aiming to be tapping in to by tapping *out* of the reliance on our human energy alone, which is limited. Useful, but not the be-all and end-all. The finite part.

Vision An umbrella term for the way you want your life to be in the future.

Wheel of Possibility A way to create structure within your whole life by 'zoning' areas of your life such as relationships, money and energetics. You can choose to pivot each zone and expand fulfilment by tapping into each of them with focus. By attending to all areas, and knowing that they interrelate, you become more whole and true to yourself and can access more possibility in your life.

ACKNOWLEDGEMENTS

To Jenni: strong, inspirational and rebellious. Never change. To Noah: may you live at the edges of what is possible for you. To Jazzy: my linen shirt man, I couldn't love you more. To my publishers, editor and agent for believing in me and being part of this transmission. To God Source Energy – whoever or whatever you are, you are glorious. To everyone in existence, for we are all here as one whole.